Phantom Law Rules

by
Troy D. Barclay

AB ASPECT Books
www.ASPECTBooks.com

Copyright © 2013 Aspect Books
ISBN-13: 978-1-57258-749-6 (Paperback)
ISBN-13: 978-1-57258-750-2 (ePub)
ISBN-13: 978-1-4796-0037-3 (Kindle/Mobi)
Library of Congress Control Number: 2012918009

Published by

AB ASPECT Books
www.ASPECTBooks.com

Dedication

To my wife, LaDonna,
for all her patience and love
and our four children
with all my love and affection
Ad Infinitum

Table of Contents

Preface

This little book is the product of reading and research concerning the favorite response of most bureaucrats, elected official, judges, and, sad to say, most common folks— "it's the law." In fact, the term "law" has many meanings. This country's laws are the direct outgrowth of one king's idea of the law as his own arbitrary whimsical decrees.

John Bouvier published Bouvier's Law Dictionary in 1859 in which he devotes about six or seven pages to the term law. But I will only quote his first part: "LAW. In its most general and comprehensive sense, law signifies a rule of action; and this term is applied indiscriminately to all kinds of action; whether animate or inanimate, rational or irrational. 1 Bl. Com. 38. In its more confined sense, law denotes the rule, not of actions in general, but of human action or conduct."

There is civil law, common law, criminal law, natural law, the law of nations, public law, private law, canon law, martial law, municipal law, foreign law, positive law, statute law, written law, unwritten law, international law, merchant law, and maritime law. But no where, no where, does this prominent 1859 law dictionary mention anything, whatsoever, about administrative law.

The purpose of this book is to examine the significance, consequences, and repercussions of this relatively new invention that is termed administrative law in modern law books. This new body of purported law is mysterious, illusive, vague, chancy, iffy, and debatable at best. It is definitely conflicting and opposite to our founding organic and original law. The question is how can this phantom law rule in a nation that is renown the world over for its rule of law and not rule by men?

Phantom law (i.e., administrative law) is a contrivance skillfully designed to enslave people via their own free will volition. In other words, it is a do-it-to-yourself concept. Voluntary effort on the part of the people as the principals, because of greed, ignorance, and/or fear, propels this purported law forward through voluntary implied or expressed contract with an agency. It has become the accepted "it's the law" under the purview of the United States' purported Civil War amendments via every conceivable, humankind invented agency.

To make it through just one day without involvement with some agency has now become a challenge for America's de jure posterity—the free white State citizen, which I refer to throughout the book. This term was used in the original, organic State constitutions, immigration laws, and early documents before the Civil War. Things changed in America with the supposed addition of the Fourteenth Amendment, which purportedly granted rights to "all persons born or naturalized in the United States," not just the free white citizens who were descendents of the founding fathers.

Before you begin reading this book, I must point out that the use of the term free white State citizen is not a racist, supremacy, prejudice, or bigotry statement. As this book will demonstrate, it is a fact in the history and early laws of America and all the individual sovereign States. Facts are facts and to write or speak about them or concerning them does not mean that someone is a racist or a white supremacist or superior in any form or fashion. We need to preserve our right to free speech and the open dialogue of ideas.

Furthermore, I need to point out that throughout the book you will see "united States of America" with the "u" lowercased. This signifies the state of the Union prior to the Civil War. The word is lowercased as it was printed in the original Declaration of Independence in 1776, where it appeared twice as "united." I believe that Jefferson and the founders wanted to emphasize that State law is the paramount law, not that of a centralized government similar to that of King George III in England, which he used against them by not allowing the colonies to have access to representation or redress of grievances. Jefferson was focusing on the individual colonies, who would become the States, who would all have representation in forming and establishing a new self-governing government where State laws would be made with the people in mind, by the people and for the people, where such redresses would be a guarantee to all their State citizens.

In all facsimiles of the original Declaration of Independence, one will note that the "u" in united States is not capitalized. But in most all of the reproductions of the text, that I have examined, the small "u" is wrongly capitalized. Thereby, people have changed or altered the meaning to adhere to today's phantom law rules system of governance. This change in spelling has confused many minds to wrongly interpret the real meaning that Jefferson and the founders had in mind. While the original Constitution of 1787 capitalizes the "U," the term "United States" has several meanings, particularly in law, since the end of the

Civil War, and one should be sure how, why, and what the term is referring to in its use in a sentence.

Likewise, in several places in this book you will also find the "s" in State(s) to be capitalized to point out that the reference signifies the use of State in the original context that the founders intended. All the State citizenry are guaranteed a republican form of government where the individual States are paramount in the legislation. (Republican is not a party, it is a guarantee in the original united States constitution at Article IV, Section 4).

The goal of this book is to examine the origins of this nation's legal system and compare it to the legal system of today. Some may feel that this book is racist or backward in nature, but please understand that my goal is to explore the early history of our country and the laws of immigration and naturalization and the State constitutions and statues.

It is my desire that this book will challenge your curiosity, interest, and inquisitiveness to find out what is actually involved in the statement "it's the law" and what concerns you should have about this baffling and frustrating phantom law. Please read with an open mind.

May the God of nature, and His Son, Jesus, the Christ, reveal to you the conspiracy that administrative law has employed and designed to destroy the united States of America. May He enable the true patriots to have an active part in the restoration of this beloved and renown common law Republic.

In His Service,
Troy D. Barclay
Perryton, Ochiltree County, Texas

Chapter I

Administrative Law and Regionalism

"Government is not reason; it is not eloquence—it is force!
Like fire, it is a dangerous servant and a fearful master."
~George Washington

"The limits of tyrants are prescribed by the endurance
of those whom they oppress." ~Frederick Douglass

The spirit and body of the common law that is unique
to the united States of America as a Christian common law
Republic was established paramount to all unborn future
bodies of law, such as administrative law, which is more
appropriately labeled phantom law today. The body of the
common law enshrined limitations in the framework of
a Constitution and subsequent Bill of Rights upon the
American government. All original State Constitutions
were written and established in conformance to this glo-
rious spirit of the law, thus making State law paramount
law.

The ideals of our founding fathers were a fundamental part of our original constitutions, laws, and early
congressional acts. No one can refute these historical
facts and laws. Laws, prior to the Civil War, were rarely enacted, which were repugnant to the Constitution.
Such de jure laws were rarely effectively challenged or

overruled as they were in accord with the original and organic founding documents.

Until the Civil War era, due process of law was strictly adhered to, but since the early 1860s the original due process under our Bill of Rights has somehow been swapped for a counterfeit due process of law under the fraudulent purported Fourteenth Amendment. Today, most laws are enacted under the auspices of this pretended Fourteenth Amendment and will not stand scrutiny under the illuminating bright light of organic judicial review. Any enactment via the so-called Fourteenth Amendment would most certainly be found repugnant, therefore null and void of any proper lawful authority.

Examine this quote and table from Sterling E. Edmunds, LL.D., professor of international law at St. Louis University. Throughout this book I quote from Edmunds' book *Struggle for Freedom*, which St. Louis University has generously granted me permission to use. Read what he says about Supreme Court cases in the chapter "The Struggle for Unitary," page 235:

> Senior Assistant Attorney General Robert Jackson, now a justice of the Supreme Court, appeared before the Senate Committee on March 11, with a lengthy statement of condemnation of the Supreme Court. He presented a complete table of the cases in which he said the Supreme Court had 'nullified' acts of Congress, not intimating that Congress might have sought to 'nullify' the Constitution in passing them:

1790–1800	0	1870–1880	9
1800–1810	1	1880–1890	5
1810–1820	0	1890–1900	5
1820–1830	0	1900–1910	9
1830–1840	0	1910–1920	7
1840–1850	0	1920–1930	19
1850–1860	1	1930–1936	12
1860–1870	4		

Concerning the constitutionally reserved field of power of the states, by the preservation of which alone may the dual balanced federal system be perpetuated and prevent the rise of an all embracing unitary national system, Mr. Jackson said: 'The Tenth Amendment, as to power reserved to the States, has not been used to assure the power of the States. It has been used to cut down the power of the federal government. Then, when those same powers are asserted by the States, the "due process clause" is used to cut down the State power. The States have no rights which the courts have been bound to respect. The State's rights argument is heard sympathetically only when pleaded by private interests in support of *laissez faire* economics to create "a no man's land" beyond the reach both federal and State power. The State's rights have become private privilege.'

When Congress says that something is prohibited, to protect you or help you, you can be sure it is the fiction of law labeled administrative rules and enforced via a form of martial law. You had better watch out, or before you know it, you will be a violator of something under this phantom law. But who prohibits Congress from being a violator of the organic Constitution of 1787? The people need to awake from their silent slumber. How is it that such phantom law exists? It can only be accomplished via martial law.

> *When Congress says that something is prohibited, to protect you or help you, you can be sure it is the fiction of law labeled administrative rules and enforced via a form of martial law.*

I heard someone on TV make this statement about a chewing tobacco regulation: "This emblem on the side of the truck, where cameras usually scan it, is something Congress prohibits." The thing that really struck me was the statement that "Congress prohibits" it. Where in the world did Congress get such power to prohibit an advertisement or to prohibit anything. A large percentage of people in prisons today who have committed non-violent crimes are there for violation of something that is prohibited by Congress. These are paper crimes of a usurped rampant renegade Congress under the guise of administrative law. People who do something that is prohibited under a regional jurisdiction of the Congress are termed "violators" and can be prosecuted and punished.

The founding forefathers of our country most definitely were not friends of administrative law and regionalism of any kind or form, nor were they supportive of any centralization of power in government. In fact, this is exactly what they were emphatically against.

Administrative law has no authoritative definition in English. The word administrative was not a word used a great deal early in this nation's history. The word "regionalism" was unheard of, let alone uttered. In fact, these words themselves, "administrative" and "regionalism," as individually defined words, are not in *Bouvier's Law Dictionary* of 1859. This administrative word is a new source of purported law, and it was conspicuously absent from most law dictionaries prior to the early 1900s. But by the early 1930s it was gathering a full head of steam to be the power behind an ugly oppressive tyrannical engine.

Administrative law is not a recognized body of American law, such as criminal law, the common law, admiralty law, or equity law. Originally and traditionally, administrative law could not be a part of our original and organic law. The federal and state de facto governments have created a new domain of governmental endeavor, embodying in itself all three aspects of our known governmental powers: legislative, executive, and judicial.

This new sphere of administrative law is proving to be a monstrous octopus, gulping up state, county, city, and citizen rights one after another. This monster is referred to by some individuals as the "fourth branch of government" and is basically a new miniature de facto government in camouflage and disguise, operating via phantom law. This created an arrogant government with its purported statutory law-making prestige, which is disturbingly unconstitutional and needs to be challenged on every front and, thereby, stopped in its tracks.

In 1936 Congress purportedly passed another renegade project known as the Federal Register Act, which provided for the printing and publication of the Federal Register. The register is published four times each week, except when legal holidays fall therein, then it falls on the day after said holidays. All administrative regulations must be published in the register before they can legally take effect.

When a new regulation is proposed, it is placed before the legislators in their legislative house boxes, and if no timely attention is asserted by the Congressperson, after thirty day, the new administrative law is printed in the Code of Federal Regulations and is given the force of law just as though Congress debated and passed such into law. Most Congresspersons never see the regulations that become de facto laws.

It seems that all any administrative agency of government has to do to "make a law" is write it up and publish it in the Federal Register. What a way for tyrants and despots to mass manufacture purported laws, i.e., phantom laws, to socially and economically control society. For an executive order to be valid, it also must be published in the Federal Register.

Read the following quote from the chapter "Administrative Tribunals" in *Struggle for Freedom*:

The minority drafted a bill entitled "The Federal Code of Administrative Procedure," providing for (1) separation of the judicial from the investigatory and prosecuting functions; (2) freedom of interested parties to appear before the agencies, with access to all information; (3) no refusal to permit an attorney to appear; (4) publication of rules; (5) notice before rule making; (6) judicial review of rules; (7) judicial review as to (a) constitutional right, power, privilege, or immunity; (b) as to the statutory authority or jurisdiction of the agency; (c) the lawfulness and adequacy of procedure; (d) findings, inferences, or conclusions of fact unsupported, upon the whole record, by substantial evidence; (e) administrative action otherwise arbitrary or capricious.

It is a curious fact that, on January 12, 1937, just, three years before the president's veto of the Walter-Logan bill, he transmitted to Congress, with apparent enthusiasm, the report of his own Committee on Administrative Management, of which he said:

I have examined this report thoughtfully and carefully, and am convinced that it is a great document of permanent importance.... The practice of creating independent regulatory commissions, who perform administrative work in addition to judicial work, threatens to develop a "fourth branch" of Government for which

there is no sanction in the Constitution
(p. 277).

Franklin D. Roosevelt was one of the strongest supporters of administrative law, i.e., phantom law, this land has ever had. He was also a traitor to organic and constitutional law. Since his New Deal, or should it be called New Steal began, phantom law grew from an embryo to a full-grown monster. Again, it is long, but it is well worth it to take a look at Roosevelt's veto of the Walter-Logan bill, which exposed his blatant, belligerent disregard for the original Constitution.

Many cases now coming before these federal boards are disposed of by "mutual consent," after an investigator has filed a secret report to which the accused is denied access; he does not know with what he might be charged. The result is a "consent order," not unusually extorted by threats or ruinous publicity and, the possible use of the full harassing power of the government, for which the victim is without redress.

In the case of one of these agencies, the Federal Communications Commission, the right of review by the courts is limited to the commission itself, where there is injury "to the public interests"; no power of review is permitted because of injury to private interests.

The overturn of constitutional principles and **the flouting of justice by these agencies caused such public dissatisfaction as** *to induce Congress to pass an act, known as the Walter-Logan bill, in December, 1940, to restore to the citizen his immemorial right to "due process of law"; that is, to appeal to the courts for redress of any invasions of his rights by the actions of these agencies. But the measure was vetoed by the president in a remarkable message, on December 18 of that year.* [emphasis added]

The message said that "the courts are not adapted to handling controversies in the mass"; that "litigation has become costly beyond the ability of the average person to bear. Its technical rules of evidence often prevent common-sense determinations on information which would be regarded as adequate for any business decision. The increasing cost of competent legal advice and the necessity of relying upon lawyers to conduct Court proceedings have made all laymen and most lawyers recognize the inappropriateness of entrusting routine processes of government to the outcome of never-ending lawsuits." The president then continued:

The administrative tribunal or agency has been evolved in order to handle controversies arising under particular statutes. It is characteristic of these tribunals that simple and non-technical hearings take the place of Court trials, and informal proceedings supersede rigid and formal pleadings and processes. A common-sense resort to usual and practical sources of information takes the place of archaic and technical application of rules of evidence, and an informed and expert tribunal renders its decision with an eye that looks forward to results rather than backward to precedent and to the leading case. Substantial justice remains a higher aim for our civilization than technical legalism....

Notwithstanding recognition of this necessity by many lawyers, jurists, educators, administrators, and the more progressive bar associations, a large part of the legal profession has never reconciled itself to the existence of the administrative tribunal. Many of them prefer the stately ritual of the Courts, in which lawyers play all speaking parts, to the simple procedure of administrative hearings which the client can understand and even participate in. Many of the lawyers prefer that decision be influenced by a shrewd play upon technical rules of evidence in which lawyers are the only experts, although they always disagree. Many of the lawyers still prefer to distinguish precedent and to juggle leading cases rather than to get down to the merits of the efforts in which their clients are engaged. For years such lawyers have led a persistent fight against the administrative tribunal.

In addition to the lawyers who see the administrative tribunal encroaching upon their exclusive prerogatives there are powerful interests which are opposed to reforms that can only be made effective through the use of administrative tribunals. Wherever a continuing series of controversies exist between a powerful and concentrated interest on one side and a diversified mass of individuals, each of whose separate interests may be small, on the other side, the only means of obtaining equality before the law has been to place the controversy in an administrative tribunal.... Great interests, therefore, which desire to escape regulation rightly see that if they can strike at the heart of modern reform by sterilizing the administrative tribunal which administers them, they will have effectively destroyed the reform itself.

The bill that is now before me is one of the repeated efforts by a combination of lawyers, who desire to have all processes of government conducted through lawsuits, and of interests which desire to escape regulation....

While I could not conscientiously approve any bill which would turn the clock backward and place the entire functioning of the government at the mercy of never-ending lawsuits and subject all administrative acts and processes to the control of the judiciary, I am of course not unaware that improvement in the administrative process is as much the duty of those concerned with it as the improvement of Court procedure ought to be the duty of the legal profession.

Recognizing this, more than a year ago, I directed the Attorney-General to select a committee of eminent lawyers, jurists, scholars and administrators to review the entire administrative process in the various departments of the executive government and to recommend improvements, including the suggestions of any needed legislation.... Apart from a disagreement with the general philosophy of legal rigidity manifest in some provisions of the [Walter-Logan] bill, I am convinced that it would produce the utmost chaos and paralysis in the administration of the government at this critical time. I am convinced that it is an invitation to endless and innumerable controversies at a private effort in the luxury of litigation.

Today, in sustaining American ideals of justice, an ounce of action is worth more than a pound of argument.

For these reasons I return the bill without my approval.

No attempt was made to pass the bill over the president's veto, the possibility of obtaining its approval by two thirds of the House and Senate appearing hopeless (pp. 271–73).

Roscoe Pound, who wrote extensively on law and social controls through law, and who I believe was in favor of Roosevelt's reforms up to a point, realized later in life that such reforms were getting out of hand. It was then that Pound wrote a reply to Roosevelt's vetoing message. He was dean emeritus of the Harvard Law School, and his reply was published in the March 1941 issue of the *American Bar Association Journal.*

In *Struggles for Freedom*, Edmunds follows Roosevelt's printed veto by quoting Pound. Though tainted with a democracy slant, it shows some principles of constitutional issues then and now as to how administrative law, i.e., phantom law rules.

All experience shows that a domain of continental extent has always been ruled either as an autocracy or as a federal government. What we have to think about, then, in this country, is the alternative of an autocracy or a federally organized democracy. We set up a federal organization of democracies with the power of politically organized society distributed between them and the federal government, and within each a parcelling out of its powers among separate departments. A federal government implies balance. It presupposes a balance of nation and State, of

23

State and neighborhood and locality of the political organization and the individual, and of the general security and the individual life. This condition of balance requires a Constitution which is the supreme law of the land; a Constitution to which all disturbances of balance can be referred and an authority empowered to apply the Constitution and restore the balance.

In other words, it requires law and law requires Judges.... There is no valid objection to rate-making or application of standards or making their own rules of procedure by administrative agencies. What lawyers do object to is the proposition that these agencies alone, of all shall be free to ignore rights; to act *in* the teeth of *evidence* or upon no real evidence; shall be free to keep the basis of their action concealed and cut off all opportunity for refuting or disputing it, and shall be at liberty to make rules of highly serious import with none of the checks which are imposed on legislative and judicial rule-making.

It is a highly gratuitous assumption, but one made frequently in lay discussions of this subject today, that administration which has always been the mode of social control by an autocracy, must be the characteristic mode of social control by a democracy. Those who would set up anew the administrative absolutism of the later Roman empire, of the French monarchy of the ancient regime, and of the administrative tribunals of the Tudor and Stuart kings, should be cautious about talking of turning back the clock. If a democracy cannot function without administrative absolutism it is fated to turn into an autocracy.

Where does this doctrine, that we must give up all checks and balances, that we may ignore individual rights, that the separation of the powers embodied in our constitutions, must be discarded, and that due process of law is an out-moded phrase—where does all this doctrine come from?... The teaching of today which encourages them, comes in one way or another from Marx's theory of the disappearance of law. This doctrine has been very heartening to the autocracies. But it is urged by teachers in the English-speaking world. There are teachers in England who object to the way in which the English Courts enforce the common-law doctrine of the supremacy of the law upon administrative agencies, and urge that the law belongs to the past and administration to the future; and this way of thinking has been growing in American institutions of learning.

Marx substituted for the interpretation of history as the record of the unfolding or realizing of the idea of liberty, an interpretation of history as the record of the unfolding or realizing of the idea of satisfying material human wants. These wants would be better and more fully satisfied when property was done away with. Rights and law to maintain them belonged to a society which maintained a regime of private property. Property and rights and law were to disappear together (pp. 273, 274).

Thus, with the passing of time, and with Roosevelt's help, the personal rule of a man has been replaced or substituted with impersonal rule of law. Man no longer can decide what is best for himself. Today he is told what to do for his benefit, such as wearing a seat belt. One is to buckle-up because phantom law so dictates.

Administrative law is a newcomer to Anglo-American jurisprudence and is hostile toward the common law. This phantom law seeks to destroy, by confounding and negating the common law's place in this country's factual historical past.

Administrative law, i.e., phantom law, was still in an embryonic stage at the beginnings of the fratricidal Civil War. It had not yet emerged from having no determinate form. It was shapeless and had not yet developed structural organization. The aggression of the faceless, nameless, and headless federal government is to disrupt the three branches and their checks and balances. Even without a constitutional amendment, all this phantom law had to do, to add this phantom "fourth branch" to the federal government, was let the weight of time and economics work. The purported passage of the three declaratory Civil War amendments with their professed power clauses effectively altered de jure organic law via voluntary self-acquiescence. Thus, through the image of a purported change in the law, a self-surrender was accomplished by a self-voluntary submission to a regional venue and jurisdiction outside the original Constitution.

The best means by which to challenge this mysterious web of deceit is to stay completely clear of it. Administrative rules are exactly akin to a spiders' web, which is spun to capture or trap its prey. Administrative law's tangled web of administrative procedure will not let you escape unharmed. You will be trapped and in a quandary if you attempt to prevail over administrative law, i.e., statutory law, with statutory law itself. It just will not work.

Black's Law Dictionary, third edition, 1933, defines administrative law as "that branch of public law which deals with the various organs of the sovereign power considered as in motion, and prescribes in detail the manner of their activity, being concerned with such topics as the collection of the revenue, the regulation of the military and naval forces, citizenship and naturalization, sanitary measures, poor laws, coinage, police, the public safety and morals, etc. See Holl. Jur. 305–307."

Black's Law Dictionary, fifth edition, 1979, refines and shortens the third edition definition to simply define administrative law as the "body of law created by administrative agencies in the form of rules, regulations, orders, and decisions."

Administrative law is currently the vehicle in use to dominate and socially control the people of this land. This was and is accomplished though subtly setting up a miniature, behind the scenes rogue government inside a government. This miniature de facto government is a big hoax and functions only under phantom law. Since the Civil War era, slowly and methodically, adoption of a form of rule under administrative regional law has perpetrated adherence to this miniature reprobate government. Administrative law has become the monopolizing body of purported law that controls most all Americans via their own voluntary obedience and submission to it. One purpose of administrative law is to destroy the common law through tricking citizens into voluntarily agreeing to give up their rights under the common law.

But the piercing question that lurks in the heart of citizens is, "Can you control human conduct with legislative statutes?" King George III of England once attempted to regulate English subjects in the colonies in America, and look what happened back then. Did the founders of this nation grant consent, acquiescence, or agreement to such rule, or did they embark upon a path to destroy forever such control over free peoples? To become submissive is to become a party or slave to the oppressive despotic ruling authority, by your own agreement.

Consent, acquiescence, and agreement by an individual must be made with an agency in order to invoke said agency's powers via administrative law. A deceptive government in miniature that uses voluntary, *mandatory* contributions and compliance is an impostor clothed with double-speak and trickery. Administrative law is phantom law.

The definition of agency as adopted by the American Law Institute is quoted and printed in the 1936 edition of *American Jurisprudence*: "Agency is the relationship which results from the manifestation of consent by one person to another that the other shall act on his behalf and subject to his control, and consent by the other to so act."

Bouvier's Law Dictionary defines agency as follows:

"AGENCY, *contracts.* An agreement, express or implied, by which one of the parties, called the principal, confides to the other, denominated the agent, the management of some business, to be transacted in his name, or on his account, and by which the agent assumes to do the business and to render an account of it.... 2. When the agency is express, it is created either by deed, or in writing not by deed, or verbally without writing.... When the agency is not express, it may be inferred from the relation of the parties and the nature of the employment, without any proof of any express appointment.... 4. An agency may be dissolved in two ways. 1, by the act of the principal or the agent; 2, operation of law. 5.—1. The agency may be dissolved by the act of one of the parties. 1st. As a general rule, it may be laid down that the principal has a right to revoke the powers which he has given;..."

> *A deceptive government in miniature that uses voluntary, mandatory contributions and compliance is an impostor clothed with double-speak and trickery. Administrative law is phantom law.*

The free white citizens are the principal. They have been duped by the fraudulent Civil War amendments and all its cohorts via alleged law such as the Social Security scheme, drivers licenses, etc. Is it any wonder why the patriot community has failed miserable to win in administrative proceedings?

In the big picture, the American people *volunteered* themselves, probably unbeknownst to them, to contract with the United States, i.e., the District of Columbia, to be their agent. Our organic rights have been traded away for mere government granted privileges. The government then acts in and for our behalf. Do you know why they say "you must" buckle your seat belt? Because its for your own safety and protection. Really? The truer fact in law is that you forfeited your rights to the *agent*—the government as your overseer for your every move. The District of Columbia is now your provider, protector, and enforcer, and everything is done for your own good and for their profit.

Proceedings before any administrative agency are strictly statutory. Any person who seeks to avail himself to such must comply with all their statutory provisions. These provisions are mandatory from the agency's point of view, and yet they have the power to exclude whatever they fancy. One must conform to each and every particular provision, such is imperative for the exercising of jurisdiction by the agency. Administrative agency proceedings are normally informal in character and are not governed by any rules suitable to official judicial court proceedings. Thus they only have a quasi-judicial capacity in which to function. They have to have people voluntarily consent, thereto, to grant this de facto body of public law any life force at all.

When application is made, invoking an agency's authority, it is not, nor can it be, governed by the rules of judicial pleading. Such formal pleadings are not essential. A statement of some significant facts is necessary for an agency to obtain jurisdiction and therewith to take legal venue before any action, such as issuing an order or rendering a decision, can take place. These facts generally do not have to be stated according to the required rules afforded pleadings in formal judicial proceedings.

There are *no* established rules of evidence that administrative agencies are required to follow. The rules of evidence that govern judicial proceedings have no authority or power in any administrative agencies' proceedings. Evidence may be presented in the form of affidavits, which includes ex parte affidavits. The powers to punish a witness for contempt is supposed to be judicial, but certain agencies are denoted to have been purportedly given this power.

Webster's New Universal Unabridged Dictionary, second edition (1983), defines administrative as "*a.* pertaining to administration; executive; as, *administrative* ability." "*n.* 1. the act of administering; direction; management. 2. the management of governmental or institutional affairs. 3. [often *A-*] the executive officials of a government or institution and their policy."

Webster's New Universal Unabridged Dictionary, second edition (1983), defines regulation as "*n.* 1. the act of regulation; the act of reducing to order, or of disposing in accordance with rule or established custom. 2. the state of being regulated. 3. a rule, law, order, or direction from a superior or competent authority regulating action or conduct; a governing or prescribed course of action." "1. (a) the division of a country into small administrative regions."

Administrative regions are simply for the implementation of administrative law, which is totally opposite to this country's original founding documents. Phantom law

31

rules primarily over people by manipulating their powers of free choice. Phantom is defined in Webster's 1949 New Collegiate Dictionary as "1. a. Mere seeming; illusion; b. A delusion. 2. An immaterial semblance, as a specter; a phantasm; apparition. 3. a. One that is something in appearance but not in reality; as, only a *phantom* king. b. A representation of something abstract, ideal, incorporeal, etc;..."

Phantom law is a ghost law. It is the mere image of real law. It has a deceptive likeness to real law. Phantom law has no real substance and is illogical to organic precepts and pronouncements of law.

> *Phantom law rules primarily over people by manipulating their powers of free choice.*

Congress is in fact the major culprit promoting phantom law with its regionalism. This is not something new. Regionalism started with military force during the Reconstruction period of the Civil War and continues today. This was accomplished through time by the buying of the votes of state legislators with public money. After the Civil War, original State constitutions were converted and/or changed. State legislators have been involved in the centralization of power in Congress, via regionalism, by passing so-called state legislation in order to obtain federal money. A prime example is the speed limit controls, purportedly to save lives and fuel. Congress promised to withhold these funds from the state coffers if state legislation was not passed to impose Congress' said speed limits. Is this not a form of blackmail?

The Civil War's purported Thirteenth, Fourteenth, and Fifteenth Amendments laid the groundwork for administrative law. Without the purported "power clause" in these amendments, none of the advancements afforded this pretended and phantom body of law would have been the least bit possible. Since the early 1930s advancements in administrative law has skyrocketed from a snail's pace to full speed ahead. Without jurisdiction voluntarily given, by people, all administrative agencies are powerless to act in any legitimate manner. Yet, agencies often act under the premise that power makes things right. Citizens, out of greed, ignorance, and/or fear, unknowingly by their own free volition grant life to this phantom de facto law.

As an example, look at the following alleged war amendments:

Article XIII

"Neither slavery nor involuntary servitude, except as a punishment for crime whereof the party shall have been duly convicted, shall exist within the United States, or any place subject to their jurisdiction.

"Congress shall have the power to enforce this article by appropriate legislation." [*Purportedly ratified December 6, 1865.*]

Article XIV

"1: All persons born or naturalized in the United States, and subject to the jurisdiction thereof, are citizens of the United States and of the State wherein they reside. No State shall make or enforce any law which shall abridge the privileges or immunities of citizens of the United States; nor shall any State deprive any person of life, liberty, or property, without due process of law; nor deny to any person within its jurisdiction the equal protection of the laws.

"2: Representatives shall be apportioned among the several States according to their respective numbers, counting the whole number of persons in each State, excluding Indians not taxed. But when the right to vote at any election for the choice of electors for President and Vice President of the United States, Representatives in Congress, the Executive and Judicial officers of a State, or the members of the Legislature thereof, is denied to any of the male inhabitants of such State, being twenty-one years or age, and citizens of the United States, or in any way abridged, except for participation in rebellion, or other crime, the basis of representation therein shall be reduced in the proportion which the number of such male citizens shall bear to the whole number of male citizens twenty-one years of age in such State.

"3: No person shall be a Senator or Representative in Congress, or elector of President and Vice President, or hold any office, civil or military, under the United States, or under any State, who, having previously taken an oath, as a member of Congress, or as an officer of the United States, or as a member of any State legislature, or as a member of any State legislature, or as an executive or judicial officer of any State, to support the Constitution of the United States, shall have engaged in insurrection or rebellion against the same, or given aid or comfort to the enemies thereof. But Congress may by a vote of two-thirds of each House, remove such disability.

"4: The validity of the public debt of the United States,

authorized by law, including debts incurred for payment of pensions and bounties for services in suppressing insurrection or rebellion, shall not be questioned. But neither the United States nor any State shall assume or pay any debt or obligation incurred in aid or insurrection or rebellion against the United States, or any claim for the loss or emancipation of any slave; but all such debts, obligations and claims shall be held illegal and void.

"5: The Congress shall have the power to enforce, by appropriate legislation, the provisions of this article." [*Purportedly ratified July 9, 1868.*]

Article XV
"The right of citizens of the United States to vote shall not be denied or abridged by the United States or by any State on account of race, color, or previous condition of servitude.

"The Congress shall have power to enforce this article by appropriate legislation." [*Purportedly ratified February 3, 1870.*]

At no time prior to the purported enactment of these amendments was Congress ever given such vast powers as implanted in their "power clauses." The history shrouding and surrounding the coercive confirmation, with blackmail and fraudulent activities of these amendments, has darkened and blemished this nation's integrity. This tinkering with the amendment process was controlled with fraud, deceit, scheming, trickery, and deception. This dabbling was purposely designed to destroy organic law and citizenship in order that the public would *voluntarily* accept such abnormal amendments as lawful.

The purported passage of these war amendments has led us, this day, to look at a seven-point summary of what is espoused by the administrative Supreme Court of the United States as the Ashwander Doctrine rules. This administrative doctrine should be studied carefully to understand where the Supreme Court has been coming from since the Civil War era. These rules are self-denying ordinances set forth in a concurring opinion in 1936, *Ashwander v. Tennessee Valley Authority*, 297 U.S. 288:

1. The Court will not pass upon the constitutionality in a friendly, nonadversary, proceeding.
2. The Court will not anticipate a question of constitutional law in advance of the necessity for deciding it.
3. The Court will not formulate a rule of law broader than the facts of the case require.
4. If possible, the Court will dispose of a case on non-constitutional grounds.
5. The Court will not pass upon the validity of a statute on complaint of one who fails to show injury to person or property.
6. The Court will not pass upon the constitutionality of a statute at the instance of one who has accepted its benefits.
7. Whenever possible, statutes will be construed so as to avoid a constitutional issue (Alpheus Mason and Donald Stephenson, *American Constitutional Law: Introductory Essays and Selected Cases*, 9th ed., 1990, p. 19).

Any challenge to the constitutionality of statutes in relationship to the original and organic law seems to be more or less derailed by this Ashwander Doctrine. But would such be possible if the American State citizens had never voluntarily traded their organic rights for government granted franchised privileges, thereby, effectively forfeiting their birthright in law? The Ashwander case speaks loud as being under the thumb of administrative law and rule.

Is the body of law known as the common law still accessible by a free white State citizen? As long as the original Constitution, which was created in 1787, is still in effect, then the body of common law can still be attained. An example of this can be found in the Supreme Court Case No. 9,375 In re Meador (1869) that one's own voluntary action can preclude one from assailing the constitutionality of a law. In said case, after a decision a writ of error was applied for, and denied, on the grounds "whereby a writ of error would not lie to a decision made by the judge in a proceeding of this nature out of court." This "out of court" statement is also discussed in the Supreme Court case of UNITED STATES v. FERREIRA, 54 U.S. 40.

Therefore, it appears that today's United States District Court judges can and often do, wear two hats—one administrative in nature as a commissioner or judge of a tribunal setting "out of court" and the other as a judge in a judicial nature or mode setting "in court." It is therefore hard, and often impossible, for one brought before said courts to determine or differentiate which type or mode of court he may be before, as the physical decor of the courtroom does not lend itself, discernible, to determine which court is which. If a citizen unknowingly acquiesces to an "out of court" situation, it appears to be construed by the court that he has "voluntarily waived venue and jurisdiction" for a judicial mode due course of the law proceeding for an "in court" redress. He has a right to due process or course of law.

It appears that this "out of court" is referring to an administrative court, commission or tribunal. "Out of court" means a court that operates under phantom law rules. While "in court" refers to a court in the nature of the original and organic concept of the law of the land bequeathed to all free white citizens in the united States of America. The lowercase "u" is purposely used to separate the "united" from the inference to the term "United States," which in law carries several meanings. The meaning of the term united States in this book refers to the original and organic concept of the Union of Republican sovereign free States that make up the American Republic Union known as the united States of America.

Thus, the courts of the united States have, since the Civil War's fraudulent amendments, become bifurcated courts. Bifurcated simply means "divided into two branches." The united States district or circuit court (in court) have been overshadowed by Congress' United States District Courts (out of court) through the bifurcated courts scheme. No one can really differentiate which is which by merely looking. Phantom law is the United States ruling law. It is totally foreign to all original and organic united States of America law.

Black's Law Dictionary, fifth edition, defines United States as follows: "This term has several meanings. It may be merely the name of a sovereign occupying the position analogous to that of other sovereigns in family of nations, it may designate territory over which sovereignty of United States extends, or it may be collective name of the states which are united by and under the Constitution." (Court cites omitted.)

The term has become ambiguous and confusing in the last eighty years or so, as "United States" as a single term is not defined even in Webster's 1828 American Dictionary of the English Language or in *Black's Law Dictionary*, third edition, 1933, nor is it defined in *Bouvier's Law Dictionary* of 1859.

The term United States of America is defined in *Bouvier's Law Dictionary of 1859*. It is lengthy, but well worth quoting as it has much bearing on the onslaught attack made by the perpetrator of administrative law and regionalism rule, i.e., phantom law, much as the tyrant King George III initiated upon the colonies. As you read the definition, think back to the time of the founding of this country and how it has evolved into the quandary and quagmire of the thought process that "it's the law" (phantom law) today. Phantom law is today's ruthless tyrant just like King George III was back then.

Bouvier's Law Dictionary of 1859 defines the "United States of America" as:

> The name of this county. The United States, now thirty-one in number, are Alabama, Arkansas, Connecticut, Delaware, Florida, Georgia, Illinois, Indiana, Iowa, Kentucky, Louisiana, Maine, Maryland, Massachusetts, Michigan, Mississippi, Missouri, New Hampshire, New Jersey, New York, North

Carolina, Ohio, Pennsylvania, Rhode Island, South Carolina, Tennessee, Texas, Vermont, Virginia, Wisconsin, and California.

2. The territory of which these states are composed was at one time dependent generally on the crown of Great Britain, though governed by the local legislatures of the country. It is not within the plan of this work to give a history of the colonies; on this subject the reader is referred to Kent's Com. sect. 10; Story on the Constitution, Book 1; 8 Wheat. Rep. 543; Marshall, Hist. Colon.

3. The neglect of the British government to redress grievances which had been felt by the people, induced the colonies to form a closer connexion that their former isolated state, in the hopes that by a union they might procure what they had separately endeavored in vain to obtain. In 1774, Massachusetts recommended that a congress of the colonies should be assembled to deliberate upon the state of public affairs; and on the fourth of September of the following year, the delegates to such a congress assembled in Philadelphia. Connecticut, Delaware, Maryland, Massachusetts, New Hampshire, New Jersey, New York, North Carolina, Pennsylvania, Rhode Island, South Carolina, and Virginia, were represented by their delegates: Georgia alone was not represented. This congress, thus organized, exercised *de facto* and *de jure,* a sovereign authority, not

as the delegated agents of the governments *de facto* of the colonies, but in virtue of the original powers derived from the people. This, which was called the revolutionary government, terminated only when superseded by the articles of confederation, ratified in 1781. Serg.on the Const. Intr. 7, 8.

4. The state of alarm and danger in which the colonies then stood induced the formation of a second congress. The delegates, representing all the states, met in May, 1775. This congress put the country in a state of defence, and made provisions for carrying on the war with the mother country; and for the internal regulations of which they were then in need; and on the fourth day of July, 1776, adopted and issued the Declaration of Independence. (q.v.) The articles of confederation, (q.v.) adopted on the first day of March, 1781, 1 Story on the Const. §225; 1 Kent's Comm. 211, continued in force until the first Wednesday in March, 1789, when the present constitution was adopted. 5 Wheat. 420.

5. The United States of America are a corporation endowed with the capacity to sue and be sued, to convey and receive property. 1 Marsh. Dec. 177, 181. But it is proper to observe that no suit can be brought against the Unites States without authority of law.

6. The states, individually, retain all the powers which they possessed at the formation of the constitution, and which have not

been given to congress. (q.v.).

7. Besides the states which are above enumerated, there are various territories, (q.v.) which are a species of dependencies of the United States. New states may be admitted by congress into this union; but no new state shall be formed or erected within the jurisdiction of any other state, nor any state be formed by the junction of two or more states, or parts of states, without the consent of the legislatures of the states concerned, as well as of congress. Const. art. 4, s. 3. And the United States shall guaranty to every state in this union, a republican form of government. Id. art. 4, s. 4. See the names of the several states; and Constitution of the United States (pp. 612, 613).

It certainly appears that since the Civil War era terminology used in concocting codes, statutes, laws, etc., has employed trickery to play on and with words. Such words purposely trick, confuse, mix up, and deceive free white people into forfeiting, voluntarily, by their own unsuspecting volition, their original and organic judicial rights to due process of the law. One can thereby be encompassed and in a quandary with such deceptive wording. Because of a person's own voluntary initiative, motivated by illusory incoherent actions, an Article III judicial "in court" proceeding becomes unobtainable and out of reach. It, therefore, appears that for a citizen to be properly before an "out of court" administrative tribunal commissioner, he/she must have entered into some form of *voluntary* consent or contractual agreement. If there is no such stipulation or nexus by which to attach to the person, then such a person is deprived of his/her judicial rights to due course of law when might or force has coerced his/her unlawful appearance in the first instance.

Can fraud, being injury to one through deception, stand on any level of agreement? There is very little in law books that address this "out of court" issue. Therefore, one should never, never, ever knowingly and/or voluntarily enter any such fraudulently induced contrivances. "Out of court" is merely a modern day inquisition for an administrative tribunal.

Administrative law is claimed to have been born out of necessity. Public opinion has been the avenue that wields, molds, shapes, and concocts statutes that give credence to and become the heart pump of administrative law. The public opinion, as to this illusive "it's the law" ideology, daily pumps administrative law's life blood throughout the nation. This necessity is only necessary under tyrannical rule of corrupted bureaucrats pursuing power and authority. They in turn pass on to the next generation of bureaucrats this twisted idea of pretended law.

To think that something as corrupt and irregular to our original and organic founding documents, as administrative law, has gained such power and prestige today is somewhat of a mystery. Its glory has come about through ignorance, fear, greed, passiveness, and a general lack of interest or understanding by an apathetic people in the basic affairs of government. Thereby, this undesirable body of law advances forward like the creeping, invincible movement of an ice glacier.

Administrative law through regulation is devouring the

stamina of this nation's youth. They are basically unaware of such voluntarism. It appears that public education is purposely or ignorantly training students not to think by or for themselves. Thus, transforming creative thinking students into regimented puppets who only know how to act when ordered by some higher administrative authority.

The process of regionalism, under any administrative form or disguise, is blatantly against and opposite to the spirit and letter of the law of the original constitution. Regionalism kindles a blueprinted path for destruction of the sovereignty of the state, the county, and the city, as well as the sovereign rights of the State citizen. It destroys all the limitations on government purposely placed there by the chains of a constitution. Phantom law purports to have somehow snapped or broken these chains.

> *Administrative law through regulation is devouring the stamina of this nation's youth. They are basically unaware of such voluntarism.*

If regionalism is not stopped in its tracks, and soon, it will destroy this nation. It appears that the only way any administrative law obtains power is through the consent, acquiescence, and/or agreement freely granted by citizens. The agreement must be made with said agency in order for that agency's jurisdiction to be conferred over the individual and operative upon him. Regionalism is the only logical method of carrying into operation the unconstitutional statutory enactments of a power hungry legislature. The illusion of law is purposely created, knowingly, by professing legislators. Therefore, if voluntary self-compliance to purported administrative agency law is not ceased—stopped right now by thousands of people—then they fail at doing their duty. A simple non-violent revolution will effectively disrupt this beastly system, causing it to die a quiet death by mere starvation from lack of subject/slave participation.

Phantom law or regionalism is slowly but surely eating away at the very core of local control of county government. Regionalism advances the idea of merging governmental functions of several counties and their cities under one head or commission. The county is the seat of government under the common law. Why is such form of republican government as guaranteed in Article IV, section 4 of the united States Constitution (1787) targeted for destruction? Such stands in the way for total control via phantom law.

Regional commissions have sought confidential information, "which they say is confidential." But will it remain confidential if such information, freely given by you, is needed, at some future point in time, to be used against you? Would you gamble on it? Washington, D.C., is subtly working hard to keep more tabs on its subject/slaves by gathering more and more "confidential information" from each individual, which is innocently and voluntarily given by unsuspecting citizens.

There are some citizens who know exactly what Congress, in concert with its empowered cronies, the administrative agencies, and regional commissions of the same ilk, are trying to accomplish with such regionalism. We cannot just stand by and watch the nation be conned into self-destructing through the voluntary forfeiture of its organic and original law.

Why or how can any administrative agency usurp our founding documents like the Declaration of Independence, (Statute of 1776), Constitution of the united States of America (1787), the Bill of Rights (1791), and the Constitution of the State of Texas (1845)? This usurper's country club seeks only complete and total destruction via its phantom law of all the organic law embodied in these founding documents.

The plan to establish the insidious regionalism in government was born via a pretended executive order #11647. Richard Nixon signed this purported order on March 27, 1969, and thus established regional government in the United States which divided the United States into ten federal regions (see Appendix C). This order purportedly merges states into new political units. This violates and is the direct opposite of Article IV of the united States Constitution of 1787. This is not a new concept, it is just rugged old feudalism in disguise.

Even the nature of the Supreme Court appears to have become administrative. Is the highest court in this land now an administrative Supreme Court? Is there a united States Supreme Court with original and organic Article III powers? I do not have the answer to the latter question. Is it really, now, a phantom Supreme Court?

How does one challenge unconstitutional acts? If governmental officials won't challenge their own unlawful acts, maybe its time to get someone in office who is not afraid to challenge these unconstitutional pretended acts being forced on us by the wolf, i.e., government, at the door. Is there one common law State citizen in office today, anywhere?

Why not say, "We, as free white American State citizens, are not voluntarily participating anymore in the destruction of this great Republic nor in its founding documents. Your administrative law stinks and I, for one, will have no party to it."

In conclusion, administrative law is phantom law. It is perverted law. It misrepresents what law is all about. It is regulation rules and not de jure law.

Illusion and delusion give it the appearance of real law. It is neither mandatory nor compulsory law. This purported law is only given credence and power through voluntarism.

Phantom law is based on fraud, deception, delusion, and is a mere mirage of law functioning only because of pretended, mandatory voluntarism. Voluntary compulsory compliance to some agency's rule is a contradicting paradox or dilemma. It is de facto government phantom law doublespeak. Is it mandatory, thus compelled, or is it unforced freedom of choice, thus voluntary? These two parts of the puzzle are diametrically opposite propositions. Thus the mind is confused, and being naturally skeptic and fearful, it will usually favor mandatory. Why? Because when something is perceived as mandatory, responsibility for some act is placed on someone other than self.

But when something is perceived as voluntary, responsibility and accountability falls heavy upon one's own self. Most every person usually seeks the path of least resistance and seeks to place responsibility and accountability upon someone other than self. This is a basic reason why phantom law is seemingly so easy and so inviting to most people. Administrative law has infiltrated every aspect of our lives and become so entrenched in our society. The best name for this relatively new phenomenon should be termed phantom law rules.

Chapter II

Voluntarism Plus Enforcement

"None are more hopelessly enslaved than those who falsely believe they are free." ~Goethe

"The world is governed by very different personages from what is imagined by those who are not behind the scenes." ~Benjamin Disraeli

Freely given consent and information is devouring this nation's freedoms, justices, and liberties on a daily basis. One day soon, this plague, known as voluntarism, will enslave an unsuspecting people. They will not even be aware that it was by their very own actions and free wills that they sealed their own oppression and have enthroned despots and tyrants to rule over them via phantom law.

The great majority of folks are apathetic to the world in which they dwell, because they are too busy trying to eke out an existence. Politics is merely something to talk about. Court is something to be avoided and hated. These folks are taught "to stay away if at all possible" or "blame the legislators for poor decisions." The key idea most people live by is "Do not get involved!"

Two of the major problems in overcoming voluntarism are greed and fear. Today, people are forced by some employers or prospective employers into a position of volunteering information and giving up their rights. Social Security numbers are a prime example. There is no law that requires anyone to obtain such a number or account. And yet practically every employer will refuse to hire a person who does not have a Social Security number or account (see Appendix A and B). Thus mandatory voluntarism is now in action. So these folks, who want a particular job, go and volunteer their information and become a part of the administrative law system. They need the benefits of the job and cannot escape the fear of not having a job, so they are trapped, like millions of other citizens, into a voluntary act that changes their status in law. They don't even realize that they no longer have rights, just mere government granted privileges.

The supremacy of economics molds the opinions that motivate voluntarism through greed and fear. Economic slaves have little desire to question how greed and fear operate upon them. The average working man has been ambushed by material struggles and is willing to sell his freedom for financial security. The "I want it" or "I need it" mentality creates a vicious pitfall that tantalizes its prey to the trap. As a member of the great silent majority, most citizens are basically apathetic to the motivation behind the necessity that purportedly hatched this administrative law, i.e., phantom law system in the first place. Most people merely follow the herd into the snare.

Let me reiterate; there is *no* law that requires one to voluntarily get a Social Security number or account. It is a mere administrative agency regulation. If you want the benefits in old age, get the number, i.e., join the agency of social security. There is no law that requires one to voluntarily use a zip code, a mere regional identifier, on first class mail. Why is it that practically all folks believe that these things are "the law"? People literally have become slaves to an illegally created fiction acquiesced to by their very own volition or free choice. They simply have believed that "it's the law" and have gone along with the crowd. This is just another nail in the coffin of disguised oppression, skillfully driven in place by the tyrants of regionalism with the hammers of trickery and deception.

If assertion of basic rights is not initiated, someday soon citizens will wake up as subjects of the District of Columbia and will find that the organic Constitution of the united States of America has been volunteered away into oblivion. It will no longer guarantee to the people a free self-government with all its guaranteed rights. These rights will have become mere abstract illusions. This nation was bequeathed such rights to freedom, liberty, and fair justice by men who knew exactly what a corrupt government can do when the chains of a constitution are broken. They wrote and spoke as voices of experience. This blatant usurpation is one of the reasons that the founding fathers so empathically despised a democracy form of government. How is such freedom, liberty, and justice lost? By voluntarily surrendering these rights to some presumed authority. Usually this is accomplished via the fears, greed, and ignorance of a docile people who unknowingly and unthinkingly do it to themselves.

Today, it seems that everywhere one looks, some administrative agency or regional commission has its fingers involved in every aspect of local government. Slowly and decidedly, administrative agencies are attempting to claim more and more involvement in our lives. Just as a termite devours its meal of wood, secretly, silently, and unseen, our government is devouring our rights. Termites, if left alone and unattended, will tumble the best built wood house, one bite at a time. By tricking, manipulating, and deceiving people, local governmental officials are causing citizens to volunteer information for far-fetched future benefits, usually in a form of monetary funds or some promised aid. When the information is given, it is like a piece of bait in a trap; there are concealed consequences and circumstances that carry a heavy price from the one caught in that trap. Anyone who invokes administrative law, this phantom law, is openly aiding and abetting in the circumvention of the original national and state constitutions.

There is a general misconception that any "statute" that appears to be "signed into law" is a lawful law. To be a lawful law and become the law of the land, any written statute must be in agreement and made in pursuant to the Constitution. A statute or law that is contrary to or violates the Constitution cannot be a replacement law. One has to be paramount and valid over the other. Both cannot carry the same force of "law."

From *Eleventh American Jurisprudence*, section 148, 1936 edition, we read the following:

> The general rule is that an unconstitutional statute, though having the form and name of law, is in reality no law, but is wholly void, and ineffective for any purpose; since unconstitutionality dates from the time of its enactment, and not merely from the date of the decision so branding it. An unconstitutional law, in legal contemplation, is as inoperative

as if it had never passed. Such a statute leaves the question that it purports to settle just as it would be had the statute not been enacted. Since an unconstitutional law is void, the general principles follow that it imposes no duties, confers no rights, creates no office, bestows no power or authority on anyone, affords no protection, and justifies no acts performed under it....

A void act cannot be legally consistent with a valid one. An unconstitutional law cannot operate to supersede any existing valid law. *Indeed, insofar as a statute runs counter to the fundamental law of the land, it is superseded thereby. No one is bound to obey an unconstitutional law and no courts are bound to enforce it* (emphasis added).

It appears that the patriot community has, for years, been barking up the wrong tree, literally. There have been struggles and battles concerning jurisdiction, common law, admiralty law, equity law, law merchant, and other assertions in courts. I, myself, have been involved in a few of these. Where did we all go wrong? Simple, we took a wrong fork in the road to justice and found that our road led to the city of injustice, where confusion, delusion, and phantom law rules. Those who seek to administer justice seem to be more interested in profit and/or elevating an ego than finding the truth. Justice has become a true phantom.

We are subjecting ourselves, unknowingly, to a system totally outside any of the tried approaches. By some

53

voluntary action on our own part, we have placed ourselves into another phantom system or purported body
of law. That body of purported law is administrative law,
created as a single, separate miniature de facto government, a fourth branch of government. Few are aware of
its existence. Some, even today, have reservations about
admitting the existence of such a counterfeit imitation
body of law.

Administrative agencies have their very own legislative, executive, and judicial powers, intertwined in each
agency's own authority. This phantom body of law is an
abusive, brazen, militaristic and domineering whimsical
system. Confusion is administrative law's illusive rudder.
One has often thought he was in a judicial setting when
in reality it was only administrative in nature and procedure, thus quasi-judicial. The decor of the courtroom did
not reveal anything to the contrary, but the judge was
just acting in the capacity of an administrative enforc-
ing judge. Thus the dilemma of judicial confusion, a true
phantom, has been created.

Here is an example of a type of foolish administrative
(phantom) rule:

> *Barclay's Statute Y X Z* - Be it enacted that
> on Mondays of each week of each individual
> year, following the enactment of this statute,
> that no person shall wear on his head a blue
> *hat* or *cap* on these designated days. This in-
> cludes, ball caps and cowboy hats.
>
> All persons shall report once a year, on
> April 1, of each following year, the number of
> times in the preceding given year, the number

of times that he/she wore a red *hat* or *cap*.

The number of times wearing of said hat or cap occurred shall be reported on form 104.

Records shall be made accessible to the appointed enforcers on their demand.

Penalty for failure to report said activity may be punishable by a confinement of up to 1 year in prison and/or a fine of $100 or both.

Penalty for wearing a blue *hat* or *cap* on Mondays may be punishable by 2 years in prison and/or a $200 fine or both.

Go to a dictionary and review the definition of shall and may. They each carry a different meaning in the interpretation of a statute. If there are statutes relating to raising and selling hogs, and if I never engage in the raising or selling of hogs, how am I made subject to that statute? Administrative law can be equaled with the illusive slang of many folks who say, "It's the law."

Nine times out of ten "it's the law" is someone's reference to some evasive comment about what they perceive law to be. My own response when someone says to me "it's the law," is, "Show me a copy of that law." Few people respond to me after my question. When someone has responded it was with some administrative code rule and not a real law. They just thought it was law for everybody.

Just what or how does one fall under a statute? What is the enabling method by which one can fall under the authority of any statute?

If I never wear a hat or cap, could Barclay's Y X Z statute affect me? Everybody is presumed to wear a hat or cap at some time in his/her lifetime. What does the word "person" mean in this statute? Can a person be defined with legal fiction as an artificial entity?

A citizen can give credence to Barclay's X Y Z statute when he voluntarily chooses *not* to *disobey* it by not wearing a blue hat or cap on Mondays. Thereby, he enables the statute to be a law that rules over him because he obeys it. He defies and challenges the statute when he *does* wear a blue hat or cap on Mondays.

The word voluntary, when used in reference to statutes, implies that one has knowledge of all essential facts. *Black's Law Dictionary,* fifth edition, 1979, defines voluntary as "unconstrained by interference; unimpelled by another's influence; spontaneous; acting of oneself. Coker v. State, 199 Ga. 20, 33 S.E. 2d 171, 174. Done by design or intention. Proceeding from the free and unrestrained will of the person. Produced in or by an act of choice. Resulting from free choice. The word, especially in statutes, often implies knowledge of essential facts. Without valuable consideration; gratuitous, as a *voluntary* conveyance. Also, having a merely nominal consideration; as a *voluntary* deed."

When you combine a rule of law, which is assumed to be true but is really false, with a person's free and unrestrained will you have, presto, rule by legal fiction or administrative law, i.e., phantom law.

A fiction of law is defined in *Black's Law Dictionary,* fifth edition, as "an assumption or supposition of law that something which is or may be false is true, or that a state of facts exists which has never really taken place. An assumption, for purposes of justice, of a fact that does not or may not exist. A rule of law which assumes as true, and will not allow to be disproved, something which is false, but not impossible. Ryan v. Motor Credit Co., 30 N.J.Eq. 531, 23 A.2d 607, 621.

"These assumptions are of an innocent or even beneficial character, and are made for the advancement of the ends of justice. They secure this end chiefly by the extension of procedure from cases to which it is applicable to other cases to which it is not strictly applicable, the ground of inapplicability being some difference of an immaterial character."

> *When you combine a rule of law, which is assumed to be true but is really false, with a person's free and unrestrained will you have, presto, rule by legal fiction or administrative law, i.e., phantom law.*

Published in 1933, the third edition of *Black's Law Dictionary* does not define this term. The definition of fiction of law is pure and simple legal jargon or doublespeak, which is exactly what the phantom law called administrative law entails!

This same language is used when you are told that the law says you have to have a license to drive or a number to work and no real harm is done when you apply for either or both. But if you are a free white State citizen, you have effectively traded your status in de jure law as a citizen for an artificial status defined person who now has only the privileges granted by a whimsical de facto rogue government. The greater weight of law and fact of consequence is that you implied that you fully understood or had knowledge of all essential facts when you signed the application. You did not bother to read, investigate, or research what you were told. You just took "it's the law" as fact. You did not challenge its constitutionality, you just accepted that it was so. Were you told all this or was it included on the application?

Go and look at a driver's license or Social Security application and see if there is any reference to your citizenship status changing from lawful to artificial anywhere on the application. That's the fraud, and it will not stand as valid in organic law. Such a contract that is saturated with fraud can be voided. When one discovers or becomes aware of said fraud, one can and should void such a contract.

If you question whether a license or application is a contract, just read the words of an administrative law tribunal judge in 1869 in the case of *In re Meador Case No. 9,375* or *16 Fed Case 1294* on page 1299:

> And here a thought suggests itself. As the Meadors, subsequently to the passage of this act of July 20, 1868, applied for and obtained from the government a license or permit to deal in manufactured tobacco, snuff, and cigars, I am inclined to be of the opinion that they are, by this their own voluntary act, precluded from assailing the constitutionality of this law, or otherwise controverting it. For the granting of a license or permit—the yielding of a particular privilege—and its acceptance by the Meadors, was a contract, in which it

was implied that the provisions of the statute which governed, or in any way affected their business, and all other statutes previously passed, which were in part materia with those provisions, should be recognized and obeyed by them. ***When the Meadors sought and accepted the privilege, the law was before them.*** And can they now impugn its constitutionality or refuse to obey its provisions and stipulations, and so exempt themselves from the consequences *of **their own acts?*** (emphasis added).

Now ask yourself the question, "What have I *volunteered* myself into" with social security, a driver's license, or merely acknowledging a zip coded address?

People came before statutes. People even came before legislatures. Tyrants love obedient subjects. Freedom is destroyed easiest by servile and spineless acquiescence.

Defiance, non-obedience, and non-observance can overturn a foolish statute and make it ineffective. People, during the last eighty years, have been coddled and cared for more and more from the cradle to the grave. This is exactly the purpose and plan of administrative law—to control via the illusion of freedom, which is in truth slavery. If necessary, the smallest amount of applied force is used to enforce voluntary compliance.

I believe that one of the goals of the Civil War was to transfer the mastery of all people, black and white, from slavery to subjection to the central government's powers, which we now know as Washington, D.C., and its fabricated war amendments (13, 14, and 15). These *power clauses* are in fact the embodied fountainhead creation of administrative law, now known as the fourth branch of government.

This fourth branch of government is in fact, at best, an extravagant preposterous counterfeit branch. In truth it is really a non-government despotic oppressive phantom scheme for social control and rule over the people. It is a de facto, rogue government.

Phantom law wants to attract all people under its domain by way of their own voluntary act, much like a magnet draws steal and metal to it.

Why did the founders not include a fourth branch of government in the Constitution of 1787? Why did they decide on just three branches of government? Were they not smart men? The pains and sufferings experienced during the ordeal of the Great Continental War taught them to be against such a phantom law control.

There are plenty of troubles surrounding the three original branches: executive, legislative, and judicial. This fourth branch, administrative, is in fact a compilation and a demented version of the three all packed into one. This fourth branch is the breeding grounds of tyrannical, despotic oppression of the worst kind. Equality and discrimination are the subtle torches that set fires of confusion, delusions, and frustrations in people. Every conceivable group of persons screams for their equal rights under the pretended Fourteenth Amendment. Under administrative law the cry for equality will never end, nor will it be settled in any satisfactory way.

As this country decays in law and order, administrative agency law is the irrefutable reason. The rights of every person are not, nor can they be or should they be the same. The second paragraph of the Declaration of Independence (statute of 1776) is often quoted and masqueraded as being the first paragraph. Most folks have no conception of what is really the first paragraph nor of its meaning and reason for being first. The "for one people" meaning has been forgotten and buried in the camouflage and deceit of administrative law.

At that time, the "one people" were the free white citizens of that day. The political body that drafted, signed, and executed the Declaration of Independence were all, each and every one, free white male English subjects. These men who were originally British subjects, declared to the world that they were *now* free sovereign citizens and no longer mere British subjects. These same citizens' descendants, acting as a group, can once again stand up for their rights and force the final destruction of all sinister administrative agency law with its regionalism.

It is most interesting that the words "enforce" or "enforcement" are *not* in *Bouvier's Law Dictionary*. Why were these words not worthy of definition in this recognized law dictionary before the Civil War? This war, in essence, forced the voluntary compliance of Washington, D.C.'s, corrupted version of law (phantom law) upon the rebel Southern States. After its end, these rebel States were enticed into voluntarily sanctioning the thirteenth, fourteenth, and fifteenth Amendments.

These amendments were passed before the South could regain their Senate and Representative seats in Congress. The representatives of the Republican States had no opportunity to engage in any form of debate for or against these said amendments. They were more or less just crammed down their throats. In other words, they were under "persuasive orders" via mandatory voluntary compliance to ratify this phantom law or else. The Northern victors thus made effective, by compelling obedience from these rebel States, submission to a phantom body of law. This phantom law was, and is, totally foreign to the organic and original founding documents. You may call it "enforcement powers" enforced by mandatory voluntarism. Is this not a skillfully disguised type of martial law rule?

> *It is most interesting that the words enforce or enforcement are not in Bouvier's Law Dictionary. Why were these words not worthy of definition in this recognized law dictionary before the Civil War?*

Now let's go back to *Black's Law Dictionary*, third edition, where we find the word enforce defined as follows; "To put into execution; to cause to take effect; to make effective; as, to enforce a writ, a judgment, or the collection of a debt or fine; to compel obedience to." If you look for the word enforcement, you won't find it. It was not worthy of a definition in this law dictionary in 1933. It appears that it was not a regularly used term in 1933 that deserved a definitive definition. Why not? Was it so new that it had no place in law terms? But when we look in the fifth edition of *Black's Law Dictionary,* which was published in 1979, there are *four* versions of these two words on page 474:

Enforce. To put into execution; to cause to take effect; to make effective; as to enforce a particular law, a writ, a judgment, or the collection of a debt or fine; to compel obedience to. See e.g. Attachment; Execution; Garnishment.

Enforcement. The act of putting something such as a law into effect; the execution of a law; the carrying out of a mandate or command. See also Enforcement powers.

Enforcement of Foreign Judgments Acts. One of the uniform laws adopted by several states which gives the holder of a foreign judgment essentially the same rights to levy and execution on his judgment as the holder of a domestic judgment. The Act defines a "foreign judgment" as any judgment, decree, or order of a court of the United States or of any other court which is entitled to full faith and credit in the state. See also Full faith and credit clause.

Enforcement powers. The 13th, 14th, 15th, 19th, 23rd, 24th and 26th Amendments to U.S. Const. each contain clauses granting to Congress the power to enforce by appropriate legislation the provisions of such Amendments.

There are *no* "enforcement powers" in the original Constitution of 1787 or the Bill of Rights of 1791. In the early days of this country, such an idea was outrageous and unheard of. This is the precise reason that the Civil War was instigated. Such poppycock, enforcement powers, is foreign to our original and organic founding documents. It is the usurper's rigorous tool of oppression used under an illusion of freedom. And this is the exact reason why the South struggled so hard to stop the District of Columbia's aggression.

Patrick Henry was very adamant about too much centralized power in government. He refused to have anything to do with the Constitution because he thought it granted too much centralized power to the government. But James Madison said that he had figured out how to limit the powers of government. He recommended limiting its power to a small land mass of ten miles square, i.e., Washington, D.C., the seat of government. (See Article I, Section 8, Clause 17 of the Constitution of 1787.)

The power clauses of the alleged Thirteenth Amendment and subsequent ones were the vehicle used to purportedly overcome these limitations set in place by the chains imposed by that organic document.

It is not so strange to find that the founding fathers were careful *not to give* Congress *too much* power. It seems that it took a terrible Civil War for some corrupt bureaucrats to purportedly alter the organic and original supreme law of the land. The skillfully hidden tool used to effect the change was martial law.

Enforcement of administrative law is accomplished because of ignorance and fear through a type of self-imposed martial law rule. There are few officers of the court, clerks, judges, sheriffs, constables, marshals, and federal, state, and city police officers who know anything except what has been erroneously "taught" or "conditioned" to believe.

What they are taught is purely administrative law. It is tragic that the common laws lie gathering dust on some top shelf, hidden and mostly forgotten. These officers of law enforcement are only schooled in enforcement tactics of the martial law rule type. In the early days there was no enforcement of paper crimes.

In fact there were no paper crimes, i.e., things that are solely legal fiction and said to be a crime, but cause no hardship or damage to another person. Originally there were no crimes of not paying taxes, as taxes were excise, import, etc., and paid when you obtained the benefit. Thus, the founders made no crime for not paying a tax. One chose voluntarily to buy something or not buy it. If he bought it, he was taxed. If he chose not to buy something, then he paid no tax. Simple system, yes, but quite different to the paper tax crimes under a system when phantom law rules.

The peace was kept by lawfully dealing with lawbreakers according to the common law. There were no tax crimes, the founders made sure of that. But that all changed during the Civil War era. People who willfully caused hardship or damage of another citizen or his property, when found guilty, paid at the hands of a common law jury of twelve peers.

Today, the problem is that all enforcement officers are trained *only* in administrative statutory regulation law. Most of these officers, if not all, know little, if anything at all, about the original and organic law of this country. This is primarily because of the paycheck rule of economics. The ones in power who write the paychecks, control and do the training.

The assumption that all people are under the powers of the purported Civil War amendments is rarely, if ever, challenged. Generations have passed on these foolish presumptions to their children, who become the next adult generation of administrative fourteenth amendment jurisdiction subject/puppets.

I am of the opinion that administrative law, functioning in mass via the ignorance and voluntary acceptance of the bulk of citizens, rules over us via the enforced power of martial law. Simply, it is hard for any policeman to accept or believe that there is no one who is not subject to this administrative law. Basically the citizenry has fully accepted this unacceptable purview of purported law. They simply lack understanding concerning the consequences of ignorance and voluntarism.

I prefer to call it enforcement power rule of administrative law. The enforcers are taught to assume that everyone has already volunteered, whether they are aware of it or not. Therefore, all are subject to be so governed.

It appears that enforcement power rule enforces only what *one* has previously "volunteered" oneself into. This term *one,* used here, refers to a free white State citizen. In this nation, as originally established, and as elaborated in the Dred Scott case of 1856–57, *only* the white race could be citizens under the supreme law of the land.

> The first of these acts is the naturalization law, which was passed at the second session of the first Congress, March 26, 1790, and confines the right of becoming citizens "to aliens being free white persons" (*Dred Scott v. Sandford,* 1856–57, 19 Howard (60 US) 393, p. 419).

Most folks have been spoon fed half-truths so long that they wouldn't know the truth if it hit them in the face. The expertise of each person is limited to only the small arena of his/her existence. People are taught early on to shun and avoid thinking for themselves. They are simply taught to be obedient and submissive to all authority. Slaves who do not know they are enslaved are a lot easier to control than ones who know that they are enslaved. Slaves who do not know that they are enslaved are more content and docile. This seems to be the real life condition in America today for most people.

If one is a police officer, etc., an enforcement officer trained only in regional administrative law enforcement, which parallels martial law, then all people are considered to be subjects under this administrative enforcement procedure. Paper crimes become the norm. Rights are disregarded daily. Human conduct is to be controlled by enforcement of legislative statutes. Is such control possible? Sure it is if everyone volunteers to be so controlled. It matters not whether citizens are manipulated, tricked, deceived, or duped into such servitude, the point and fact in law is that their own free act of volition is controlling them. They volunteered! They, for all practical purposes, enslaved themselves.

The way to end this servitude is to stop volunteering and start asserting the organic and original law. Did you *voluntarily* obtain that license or account? It matters not what motivated you, you *volunteered*. If the inducement was perpetrated by fraud, deceit, and/or deception, the contract is voidable by the principal.

There is a collision course set between administrative law and organic law that is inevitable. It shall happen sooner than later. When the idea that the people have been had through "voluntarism" is exposed, a revolution will ensue. This new regime in law (administrative law) will self destruct. The salient organic law will prevail in the end. The despotic kingdom set up through the years via the darkness of administrative agency law will suffer a catastrophic collapse. Restoration of the great common law Republic will be accomplished by the descendants of the original forebears. Phantom law will no longer rule, when ignorance, greed, and fear are dispelled in the lives of the citizenry.

There is a zoo in Fort Worth, Texas, that I once visited, where, to view the live bird life, you walk through a dark passage into their well illuminated cage. There are no screens or fences to keep the birds from flying away and escaping into freedom. They are free in the big cage to fly anywhere, even into total freedom. It is their fear of the darkness and their mental capacity that enslaves them. They fear the dark so much that they keep away from the darkness. They believe that there is no way to escape, so they never attempt to flee.

But the truth of the matter is that the birds, one and all, could fly into the real world of total freedom. All they would have to do is venture through the short passage of darkness through which all visitors walk in. There are no screens or wires or any visible or definable restraints to stop them. It is just their belief that they should not fly toward the darkness that stops them. Thus, they are enslaved. If enough light was placed in the darkened passageway to equal the light in the caged area, they would fly away to freedom.

Today, it is the dark passage of greed, ignorance, and fear coupled with people's voluntary acquiescence to their condition of servitude that chains them to this phantom law tagged as administrative law. A wretched government who is possessed of an uncontrolled power, i.e., phantom law, is simply the manifestation of human greed coupled with violent enforcement of mandatory and compulsory voluntarism.

The prejudices and repulsiveness of most well-to-do folks toward law, morality, religion, and politics will change drastically. The working person will once again shed their greed and ignorance and educate themselves in all these matters that have captured and duped their mind. Fear will then disappear. Epic change will come quickly and positively. Administrative law, the illustrious phantom law, will evaporate under the exposure of thought, reason, and common sense of an enlighten citizenry.

Part of the fuel that fans the flames of phantom law and has since the 1930s is that the higher institutions of learning the law have advocated that no one study the Constitution for it is "horse and buggy law" that would be apt to "confuse their minds."

Knowledge and understanding will displace fear, ignorance, and greed. They bring courage and strength in character. Confidence is regained with these two qualities. The shackles produced by administrative economics will be broken. Knowing the truth sets one free. The truth is truth whether anyone is aware of it or knows it to be the truth or not. When knowledge is attained and the light of truth shines bright concerning the phantom law, economic slavery will have to crumble and disintegrate.

The only solution that can bring peace to individuals is in their overcoming of ignorance. That is one struggle in itself. But, if people would stop *volunteering,* and thereby

69

invoking the jurisdiction of some agency's administrative law enforcement powers, this mess would go a long way in unraveling itself. There needs to be a course of study in voluntarism for folks to become educated of its consequences.

There are three methods that prompt folks to volunteer into this administrative phantom law. Either they volunteer for some monetary reward (greed). Or they volunteer out of a belief of future punishment (fear) if they don't volunteer. Or, lastly, they are told and tend to believe the hearsay that "it's the law" (ignorance).

There are few who desire to be educated in the principles contained in the original founding documents of our nation. They have been taught so long that in their mind they view such documents as having been "changed." But by what? The enforcement powers of the alleged amendments? Time will one day verify that the pendulum is coming back, ripe for the restoration of the Republic. The clock of time is ticking away, minute by minute, day by day, and year after year.

The following quote was spoken by Frederick Douglass in 1857:

> Those who profess to favor freedom and yet deprecate agitation, are men who want crops without plowing up the ground. They want rain without thunder or lightening. They want the ocean without the awful roar or its waters. This struggle may be a moral one; or it may be a physical one; or it may be both moral and physical; but it must be a struggle. Power concedes nothing without

a demand. Find out just what a people will submit to, and you have found out the exact amount of injustice and wrong which will be imposed upon them; and these will continue till they are resisted with either words or blows, or with both. The limits of tyrants are prescribed by the endurance of those whom they oppress.

Tyrants and despots have always pressured and oppressed those who would not *voluntarily* submit to their whimsical decrees, judgments, and rules. Many patriots have suffered throughout history for their refusal to willfully volunteer. So goes the world today! We hope and wish to be left alone. We cause no hardship or damage, yet the enforcers believe that all people can be whipped into submission. The fear of jail or prison curtails most folks, sufficiently. But there are the few who, because of their stand, always have been and always will choose freedom, liberty, and justice, even at the high expense of wrongful incarceration, or even death, by renegade tyrants and despots along with their ignorant cronies.

Has this picture changed much today? No! The struggle for freedom goes on day by day. Problems of unlawful restraints upon some patriots' liberties are inevitable and sure. But as the resounding immortal words of Patrick Henry—"Give me liberty, or give me death"—still breathe life into many patriots. There will always be citizens who assert their unalienable God given rights, no matter what it costs.

Chapter III

Common Law Dead! Says Who?

"Justice is itself the greatest standing policy of civil society; and any eminent departure from it, under any circumstances, lies under the suspicion of being no policy at all." ~Edmund Burke

"Resolved, N.C.D. 5: That the respective colonies are entitled to the common law of England, and more especially to the great and inestimable privilege of being tried by their peers of the vicinage, according to the course of that law." ~Declaration of Rights, 1774

To say that the body of law known as American common law has been taken over or replaced is to say that the Christian Republic established as the united States of America is no longer in existence. This is a lie, one that is in, itself, maybe aiding and abetting the destruction of the Republic.

If some body (legislature, etc.) passes a law that you can't wear a blue hat on Mondays, the law stands as a statute and stands as in law until some citizen challenges and/or breaks it. Now, if the person is on a ship (admiralty), inside a fort (territory), or wants the benefit of being equal with his neighbor (equity), then such a citizen could likely loose his/her case, but if he is a free white citizen, he can invoke the law of the land under the common law of the Constitution (1787–1791) and can win because of that standing of citizenship in law. His wearing of a blue hat cannot cause hardship or damage to anyone. Nor does the government have the right to enact such a frivolous unconstitutional statute.

If some code like the Uniform Commercial Code or Internal Revenue Code, is unconstitutional, then it cannot be law, as it never could be regarded as having the power or force of the Constitution behind it in the first instance. It is in fact and law null and void of any lawful, binding authority upon any actually citizen. The only way people become subject to such codes is to voluntarily place themselves under that code or when martial law is imposed.

The facts are mostly misinterpreted by patriots. Codes like the IRS, EPA, and all other groups of the same ilk, along with their decisions are constitutional under the United States Constitution (amendments 11–26), as has been held by its administrative Supreme Court. But remember this is not under the original united States Constitution of 1787. These codes and decisions are held constitutional under the enforcement power clause de facto United States Constitution, i.e., purported amendments 11 through 26.

There is no way on this earth such codes or decisions could ever be held to be constitutional under the original founding document's of law for our country. No court case has ever challenged, effectively, the constitutionality of these amendments, except possibly the Eighteenth Amendment, and it was purportedly overturned.

Today, everyone is presumed to be under the jurisdiction of the United States Constitution primarily via its declaratory Fourteenth Amendment. But how can people place themselves under a code to begin with if they are not volunteering to such? I believe that citizens can place themselves under the enforcement rules of administrative agency law if in fact they are found to have some voluntary attachment to the democracy system via the Fourteenth Amendment, Social Security account or number, license, and any like contrivance. No statute can be law, at anytime, if it is unconstitutional under organic 1787–1791 documents.

> ***Paper money is fiat money. Its value fluctuates and changes constantly.***

Most statutes today claim such lawful authority in the democracy via the District of Columbia's constitutional power clauses. When one has consented to being a subject/slave of the District of Columbia, he has little recourse and absolutely no lawful redress of grievance. There cannot be a substantive constitutional law under democracy rule. Some say that by trading the Federal Reserve's paper money one has volunteered into such a brute system. How can an artificial person (corporation) circulate anything? Such cannot walk, talk, nor write its name. To say that an artificial person (corporation) can circulate something is pure legal fiction. Lawful money *can* be lawfully circulated by lawful, de jure, common law citizens or anyone who is alive and walking, talking, and breathing. Paper money truly lacks substance, because true intrinsic substance does not exist in such a form of mob hysteria. The lack of understanding concerning coin, circulation and credit leads to serious economic problem for any country. Thus phantom law slips and slides quietly into place.

This nation was established and erected as a Christian common law Republic, not a mob rule. A democracy is defined as mob rule. Federal Reserve notes are evidences of debt of the Federal Reserve corporation. Said corporation is a large conglomerate that circulates paper notes for a commodity. If a majority of people would stop circulating this fiat paper note, it would cease to exist.

If I give nothing (paper money) for goods and services, how can this invoke any body of law; unless the person who sold (gave) me the goods decides to file theft charges, in common law, against me? But how could he when he voluntarily gave it to me?

Paper money is fiat money. Its value fluctuates and changes constantly.

I have the view that if I have nothing of intrinsic value (paper money), then I can give nothing to anyone else, even if that person *is* willing to exchange with me my *nothing* for his *something*. Value, outside of lawful coins, can only be established by the parties involved in the transaction, not the legislature or the courts. Lawful coinage is provided in the Coinage Act of 1792 via Article I, Section 10 of the united States Constitution of 1787. The usurped application to paper money can only function by voluntarism via the purported Fourteenth Amendment, which is brazenly unlawful under organic law. If America would suddenly stop taking, trading, or dealing in Federal Reserve notes, their circulation would stop *in* its tracks.

Common law free white State citizens cannot be compelled into code compliance (statutory rule) except by their own volition or voluntary act. If the people are the government, then who has allowed a usurped government to deprive any lawful citizen of the common law? If government is doing that, then that renegade government has become the monster or master and the people are its slaves. Then, if I consent to it, I deprive myself access to lawful law, therefore, the phantom law has me in its grasp.

Some say that the body of law known as the common law is dead! The common law body of law may be wounded, but it is *not dead*. It has not been executed yet. Codes, merchant law, international law, or martial law cannot fire the death bullet to the common law body of American organic law. They may inflict pains and oppressions, but not death.

Our forefathers knew all about the common law, law merchant, admiralty, equity, and martial law. They knew full well that if such phantom law was conceived, it would give birth to corruption and forever be pregnant with despotic and tyrannical oppressions. They knew absolutely everything about the, then, unborn administrative law, i.e., phantom law type of militaristic, authoritative system of law. They were disgusted with oppressive rule by tyrants and despots who rule parallel to administrative law. They wanted to seal forever any conception and birth of any such de facto system of domineering rule.

Under this brazen and unwanted authority, the "rulers" or "powers that be" are illusive, and it is hard to point out any breathing real-live culprits. The original founders wanted to set a free de jure government in force that covered all forms of law in their proper places. Administrative law is dreadfully alien to our original and organic laws. To be free and self-governing, one must have knowledge of all the different bodies of law. I have to know the law and what body of law I, myself, invoke over me via my own voluntary acts. I need to realize the consequences of my action if I do volunteer or if I don't wish to volunteer. The founders were on watchful guard against any type of what we now call administrative tribunals under phantom law rules.

Today, in the united States of America, this phantom "they" has tried to build the "fort" (Art. I, Sec. 8 cla. 17) wall around the outside perimeter of the united States of America, thereby placing everyone "inside the fort" and under that body of law now known as "regional administrative law" via enacting purported "legislative territorial law." During the Civil War time full martial law was imposed and maintained until well after the reconstruction era. Some believe it is operable even today. But where are the tanks and troops that force enforcement? Could these "troops" be the local and corporate state "police force"?

When I fly in an airplane, I, myself, invoke admiralty law by getting on board. Admiralty law is there all the time, operable upon all who board the plane. It is proper, as I want the captain to pilot the plane. I do not want him to let just any passenger at the controls of that plane. But when I get off that plane, the captain no longer has any say or command over my performance, *unless,* I don't want to be responsible for my actions and *grant* to him, voluntarily, the power to continue to command performance over me, which would be stupid of me. To say that I granted the captain of the plane, jurisdiction over me when I got the ticket (some say that having a paper [Federal Reserve] note) is what negotiable instruments are—tickets—is pure nonsense.

The mere fact that you have a ticket in your possession does not compel you aboard admiralty law. The ticket only grants permission to board the plane. I have to walk onto the plane to invoke admiralty law over me. Where and how can one say that I boarded such a ship or airplane with the purchase of a ticket with paper money? I can trade my plane ticket(s) to you, for you to board that admiralty flight (law), but if I in fact never get aboard the plane, have I invoked any admiralty law by having it in my possession? I think not! Just the common law of ownership. The airplane may land in every state, but I do not have to get off or board it. I can sign my airplane ticket, so what does that mean? Nothing! There is a place for all the different bodies of law and their proper jurisdiction.

My airplane ticket obligates me to nothing, *unless,* I demand it. The airline cannot compel me to get aboard, without exerting force (full martial law), but if I so choose, the airline will honor its obligation. If I never use the ticket, who profits? The airline "thinks" it makes a profit, because it never had to perform, yet they received the Federal Reserve note or *nothing.* If I sign nothing to get the "ticket" or trade the Federal Reserve notes, what thing or who can make me use it?

The airplane ticket may be in my hands, but *unless* I physically walk on board, I do not and cannot invoke admiralty law. I, however, invoke the common law right to possess even a worthless piece of paper. How can we be so stupid to allow someone (the captain) to dictate to us how we should act or move when we are outside of his jurisdiction and venue? The free white citizen in this country has to bow to no person or entity, whatsoever; as he is king of his castle, as long as he doesn't go *outside* the law by causing hardship or damage or voluntarily trading his common law birthright for some government granted privilege.

Negotiable instruments *cannot* be the contract; they are only tickets to contract through. If someone claims such, then void the contract. No contract can stand when saturated with fraud, deceit, deception, coercion, and duress.

If I should get off the airplane in another state, I can invoke the common law. If I cause hardship or damage, I am responsible for my actions and/or inactions while I so sojourn in that state. I can also invoke the common law of possession if I purchase something. You have to voluntarily invoke a relationship with some administrative system or agency, yourself, in order for said agency to be able to assert any jurisdiction.

Why has the IRS stated for years, and as far as I know, still openly use such phrases, "Voluntary self-assessment" or "voluntary compliance"? Why do we not pay attention to what agencies and their laws are really telling us?

I believe you make the *record* in common law; therefore, your record must of necessity be filed with the county clerk or recorder of such records in the county in which one's place of abode is found. Notice of that record is essential and must be served upon known parties that may have an interest.

Some espouse the position that the entire country, i.e., the District of Columbia, is operating outside the constitution under international law (private law). It can't be! If *one*, just one, free white American State citizen at common law is still relying upon the original and organic Constitution (1787–1791), it *is* still in force and paramount law. We, the people, must assert our rights under said organic Constitution *or* the so-called democracy, with its enforcement power clauses, towers above our blessed Republic. I for one will not acquiesce to my own destruction or the destruction of our profound original Constitution. The artificial cannot rule over the natural, its creator!

At one point in time special appearance possibly was used in a de jure (in court) court setting in the national judiciary that is covered in Article III of the united States of America Constitution. Why go into their private courts, except by special appearance?

> *This phantom law is ghost law and that is exactly why it scares so many folks into voluntary compliance.*

But special appearance is nonexistent today in administrative law. The issue is settled before you appear in the first instance. You volunteered into the vicious system or you would not even be making any kind of *voluntary* appearance in the first place. How on earth can you expect to make a special appearance to tell them they have no jurisdiction over you? How frivolous and preposterous!

A lawful court cannot overrule constitutional arguments properly laid out under standing of common law status. But you cannot claim the common law when in fact you have placed yourself under regional administrative (phantom) law; for you have effectively removed yourself from the protection afforded under common law basic rights, for an "in court" redress of grievance, and you have done it voluntarily. When you volunteered, you asked for some future benefit or protection or help from the administrative law. There is no place for the common law in administrative law. They are direct opposites. Common law has provisions for redress of grievances. Administrative law has no such provision, just whatever whim they want to grant to you per their edicts.

Some say that to file notices and documents in the county records means nothing under code rules. It may not. But, it *does* have meaning at law. And that is what I am primarily concerned with. Why should I waste time studying and performing under their codes, rules, and law of their private administrative agencies, nor should I believe such to be superior truth and/or fact. Herein is the bigger con game—to get me to believe that common law is dead! Do we only have administrative law in force today? I think not! The American common law is the paramount law of this union. All the de facto phantom administrative rules in the world cannot change this fact.

Phantom law cannot replace the common law, the admiralty law, or equity law. This phantom law is ghost law and that is exactly why it scares so many folks into voluntary compliance.

The only way to invoke a jurisdiction outside your status as a free white citizen in the united States of America is to invoke the Fourteenth Amendment, Social Security account or number or any license or some other similar contrivance by volunteering or consenting of your own free will volition. Such free white citizens cannot be forced or coerced into such artificial status against their free will. Any such forceful coercion against a free white citizen is a full fledged martial law type operation. If this type of martial law rule is in full force in this country, then there are no sovereign States. Regionalism under martial law will have replaced them.

No person or government can own me *unless* I consent to such legal fiction. I have never agreed nor stipulated to such artificial character, knowingly or voluntarily, nor will I.

Without attachments or nexus to the democracy (Washington, D.C.'s regionalism administrative municipal legislative law—enforcement under martial law, if necessary), the Republic is still in existence and is functional. The lie that the Republic is dead, is just that—a lie. To believe such a lie and spend all your time studying democracy codes is aiding in the scheme to destroy our blessed Union of Republican States. Please study for yourself and interpret the common law documents— The Statute of 1776 (Declaration of Independence), the Constitution for the united States of America, and your original State constitution.

There is hope for the restoration of the American common law Republic. If that hope dies, we all perish. Freedom, liberty, and justice that once thrived feverishly in this nation will disintegrate also. Free self-government will vanish from this great earth if common law dies in this land. The last frontier is under siege. This land is being raided and ravaged by this illusive phantom law rule.

We must protect freedom, liberty, and the pursuit of happiness under the original and organic documents of this nation and our States. It's the only real and logical answer. It is our duty to stop the vicious regional administrative law, which is known as phantom law, before it destroys our Republic.

Étienne de la Boétie wrote the following in *A Discourse on Voluntary Servitude:*

> All this havoc, this misfortune, this ruin, descends upon you not from alien foes, but from the one enemy whom you yourselves render as powerful as he is, for whom you go bravely to war, for whose greatness you do not refuse to offer your own bodies unto death. He who thus domineers over you has only two eyes, only two hands, only one body, no more than is possessed by the least man among the infinite numbers dwelling in your cities; he has indeed nothing more than the power that you confer upon him to destroy you.... Resolve to serve no more, and you are at once freed.

Chapter IV

Court—an Arena

"I believe there are more instances of the abridgement of the freedom of the people by gradual and silent encroachment of those in power than by violent and sudden usurpations." ~James Madison

"Justice without power is impotent, power without justice is tyrannical." ~Pascal

"Laws are a dead letter without courts to expound and define their true meaning and operation."
~Alexander Hamilton

The tragedy of our court system today is that it has departed from what our founding fathers envisioned as the concept of justice for a self-governing people. The travesty is real. The perversion is nearly complete. Regional administrative law, or phantom law, which is a deceitful form of injustice, reigns by way of despots, tyrants, and so-called judges—men and women who are subverting our original organic judiciary.

They are accomplishing this by plummeting justice, through trickery and deceit, into deep dark cages. They, the judges, are the trainers or "masters" who keep, and often hide, the keys to all the ball parks or jurisdictions.

They (judges) are attempting to keep the American common law locked up tight and on a high shelf where it will gather the dust of time.

Two keys to this dilemma are knowledge and courage. They dispel ignorance and fear. Most judges claim or acquiesce to the fact that the very system or body of law that established this great nation is now only an worn-out antique, obsolete for a modern society. A new regional administrative enforcement law rules supreme. This is the dominant body of purported law that today governs with tyrannical authoritative power. This phantom law punishes all violators whimsically.

> *The tragedy of our court system today is that it has departed from what our founding fathers envisioned as the concept of justice for a self-governing people. The travesty is real. The perversion is nearly complete.*

What has caused or allowed this? Why was such allowed to happen in a short 235 years since the birth of free government? How did this phantom law get its foot in the door in this nation? What has happened to a trial by jury of one's peers? Who is responsible for such perversion? The Civil War's purported amendments supposedly gave a new slant to due process or course of law. Sure, judges possess a part of the blame, but only a part. The people are at fault. Yes, you and I are the big cause that allows injustice to reign and be maintained. Voluntarism has elevated administrative law to a sort of kingship. We, ourselves, have allowed the hall of our temples of justice (courthouses) to be invaded, thereby corrupted. We, ourselves, have allowed this travesty through apathy, fear, ignorance, passiveness, and voluntarism.

Let us attempt to unravel what has brought us to this point. Why has it happened? What laws keep this engine of oppression running in today's real world? I hope to also show that there is a way out of this mess. There is hope! Americans think they are free, yet they are being ruled deceptively by an illegitimate democracy run by usurpers. It is called rule by fiction of law, i.e., phantom law. It is basically rule under falsehoods, lies, or fiction, and it is nourished and thrives on voluntarism.

The best analogy for a layman who has little knowledge of the "law" but wishes to understand today's court system is a wrestling arena where a wrestling match takes place.

The whole wrestling match is staged. It is fake; it is make-believe. It is a contrived and rehearsed performance or show. The bout or "match" gives all appearance as to make the spectator feel that it is real and harsh pains are inflicted. In wrestling, all wrestlers pretty much know each other; they may even be friends. They may even ride to the arena in the same car.

The public, through well dramatized promotional publicity, is conned into thinking that one opponent is really going "to work" the other opponent over. Fanfare sympathy performances, exhibited in advertisements, are espoused for the underdog. Good guys versus bad guys acts are promoted long before the actual wrestling match.

It appears that the referee often attempts to keep chaos from prevailing. But in reality, it is a rigged performance in the art of deceit and fraud for a profit. For all wrestlers earn their living with such performances. The "match" is an exercise in controlled anger and pretended physical abuse for profit. And yet people pay to watch and be a part of this farce. No one has to get into the ring or arena or be a spectator, he volunteers.

The same holds true for your "day in court." It is a "match" between attorneys who use controlled expressions of staged anger toward opponents so each client "thinks or feels" that he/she is getting his/her money's worth. The attorney, all to often, is putting on a show for money or profit. Venue, in its legal ruling sense, is seldom questioned, nor is jurisdiction rarely questioned by attorneys because that does not result in a good profit.

Citizens are assumed to have placed themselves under the venue and jurisdiction of the regional administrative law. The courts for this fabricated phantom law will be used, when needed, to enforce agency laws. The spectator client or just plain citizen will be tricked into granting, voluntarily, jurisdiction to this phantom law any way possible. The apex of this foreign body of purported law feeds on voluntarism. So the attorneys play the legal game for the rewards.

To me, this is a perfectly vivid picture of today's courtroom scene. Performances by judges and attorneys are like the wrestlers and referees, just a big fake. The real "winners" are both of the attorneys. They often reap huge profits, or a better term might be legal plunder. The real "losers" are their apathetic and submissive clients. They pay and pay. They hire an attorney, believing he will really fight for their "point of view" or "rights." The other side does exactly the same thing. And if the other side is the state or government attempting to prosecute you, you then have the privilege to pay both ways. You pay for your defense and also you help pay the salary of the government personnel. If you choose to represent yourself, you are treated as a fool

The courtroom scene or "day in court" is usually really not what each client thinks it is going to be. Clients usually think that such is a place where justice will prevail. That is simply not so, it is justice for *none*, except maybe, for the paid administrators.

To each client's dismay, I believe the scene is lawyer versus lawyer in front of a judge who can control them both. The judge may let it get fairly heated before he/she calls for one or both of the lawyers to settle down. The clients have no way of knowing that the courtroom scene they are experiencing was most likely previously rehearsed in a conference room or club or bar over a drink or two with the two attorneys and judge discussing what will be said and actually acting out what will happen on the stage during the final scene in court.

Furthermore, I believe that the judge, more than likely, has already told both attorneys, who are officers of "his court," what to get their clients to agree to between themselves, before they come back into the courtroom. This relieves the judges from positions of responsibility and accountability. The clients have agreed already, in advance, or at least the attorneys have "worked" out some voluntary plan that all agree to.

This is exactly what a plea bargain deals with. A plea bargain is a coerced voluntary acceptance of some deal.

It gives the appearance of justice but is in fact the injustice produced by the egos of some prosecuting attorney and usually a public defender. Clients are often forced to voluntarily accept a deal to lessen what they surmise and are told will be their sentence. Innocent people, out of fear of the unknown, or ignorance and/or for money questions, often volunteer themselves into being labeled or classified as a criminal. They are tricked into accepting a blemish on their reputation and administrative records via their confessed lesser crime, one that they are really innocent of ever committing in the first place. All such havoc is an imitation of justice and only serves to advance the idea of phantom law rules and the pocketbooks of its administrators and the elite powers that be.

> ## *The courtroom scene or "day in court" is usually really not what each client thinks it is going to be.*

Usually out of the clients' own mouth comes deadly and fatal damage to their cause. Clients usually agree to a plea bargain or settlement. The attorneys relay their client's agreements to the judge, and the judge rules accordingly. People have a tendency to talk too much. People often develop a severe case of oral-diarrhea when confronted with a legal issue. They mistakenly believe they have to volunteer information to win their case or save their own hide. They believe they can talk their way out of this or that. Most often "mouthing off" only serves to deepen the problem.

Justice has not prevailed, only the power and law of motivation and/or negotiations have finally pinned one of the opponents to the floor for the final count. After the final judgment, the losing client may say, "I should have had a better attorney, or done a better job myself, or if only we had gotten this or that evidence admitted, we would have won." Clients also may say, "My attorney really made them squirm" or "Well, we had our day in court." Regardless, both clients feel emotionally relieved on the one hand and/or distraught on the other hand.

Of course, in my opinion, it really makes no difference whatever excuse is offered, it would not have mattered one iota. The case rested upon the whims and moods of the judge, attorneys, and/or the client's pretrial agreements. Possibly judgment could have been swayed by an opponent's argument by one of the attorneys. Unfortunately, I believe that the determining factor quite possibly can and is often swayed by the size of one's pocketbook. If that premise is true, then so-called justice is for sale, and the poorer person hasn't much of a chance at any justice. The common person's best ammunition on this legal battle is knowledge in organic and original law and to stay away from attorneys.

A spectator from the area surrounding the wrestling ring is *not* a person wrestling in the arena. He is not automatically placed under the administrative law venue and jurisdiction of the fight ring unless he has placed himself there beforehand by some voluntary act. He has not been trained in how to take a fall or to kick the opponent without really inflicting harm or hurt. He has not been trained in defrauding and deceiving the picture being portrayed to the public. That is how to make people think he has

90

inflicted extreme pain, when in reality there was little or no pain inflicted. He also has not been trained in how to make the people think a blow he suffered was to the point of being unbearable when really it didn't hurt at all or very little.

The arena, administrative law, i.e., phantom law, in a more general sense, really includes the whole region of the building area. Once you bought a ticket for the match and physically walked into the building, you inadvertently placed yourself, voluntarily, under the relentless regional administrative law enforcement with all its powers pertaining to this match or as long as you remain on the premises.

Simply put, I believe the courtroom scene or wrestling arena, is all acting, an exercise in staged fake. A performance designed and rehearsed to play upon the ignorance, fear, emotions, and voluntary participation of the spectators to plunder their financial pockets.

No truer analogy or allegory can be drawn than that today's courtroom scenes are designed to function just like a fake wrestling match. The sad tragedy is that a wrestling match does little harm to the spectator, while our court system is ruining, devastating, and breaking the client emotionally, financially, mentally, and spiritually every day.

This illegal plunder must be stopped. Knowledge and correct education in how to *not* be a volunteer will stop regional administrative law in is tracks. Clients who have had their day in court often feel outraged, cheated, tricked, railroaded, etc. The very fabric that binds this nation together is being torn into shreds and pieces, unraveled daily by the corrupt, bias, and arbitrary quasi-judicial system and the decisions made by judges and lawyers, which appear to be primarily motivated by greed. The justice that once was prized so highly by all spectator-clients is wounded, if not dying. The court-houses across America, where justice reigned in all her truthful proceedings, dressed in integrity, honesty, fair-ness, truth, and morality, have been invaded by power, corruption, deception, lies, trickery, fraud, dishonesty, and immorality. Thus, all we have today is quasi-judicial, phantom law, proceedings.

> *This illegal plunder must be stopped. Knowledge and correct education in how to not be a volunteer will stop regional administrative law in is tracks.*

The common law system of jurisprudence that made America a Christian common law Republic is being con-sumed by greed, pride, envy, fear, and ignorance. These cancers of the human nature will be fatal if not diagnosed and expunged from the system.

Our judicial system has been tampered with to the point that lawful judicial process has been stopped in its tracks. This is what the Civil War bequeathed to us.

Our judicial system, today, is like a tractor-trailer rig that has a powerful engine, transmission, and eighteen wheels. Fully operable, it can pull and move heavy loads up steep mountains. Fully operable, our common law system of jurisprudence meters out, under the wisdom of twelve free white men who were all property owners seated as jurors, judging both the law and the facts—this is justice that is truthful, honest, and most usually fair and impartial.

But if you take a tractor-trailer and put it at the bottom of a mountain with twelve flat tires, a shorted out starter, and stripped gears, it will not move at all, for it cannot even be started. Hence, it must be repaired by a mechanic in a garage capable of such repairs before it will move any load up the mountain. The mechanical system is there, it always has been; however, it is in need of urgent repairs. If such repairs are performed, the tractor-trailer (otherwise known as the judicial system) will be operable once again.

The question is who can repair the common law system of jurisprudence? The answer is the descendants of the founders.

It is assumed that most who read these words are descendants of the founders or have been a spectator-client in some capacity. Spectator-clients will have to find a way to protect themselves in the court arena. A serious study of law is a must. This little book, I trust, will hopefully serve as a spring board into that pool of knowledge and understanding and aid in the restoration of American justice, keeping you out of the tangled web of the stern regional administrative law. My goal is to challenge everyone to gain such knowledge in order to dispel fears and ignorance of quasi-judicial and political pitfalls that daily affect our lives. I hope that even someone well versed in the law will gain a deeper understanding of our system of jurisprudence. We need to better understand the illogical system of administrative law, i.e., phantom law, that is subtly being established as the new body of law. Since the 1930s this new "sociological jurisprudence" has been substituting its phantom law, i.e., regional administrative law, for the common law.

Martial law is not really a body of law—it has no book of doctrines or procedures. A method of "social control" that works through the existing legal machinery whenever possible has purportedly found its place in this land. This "social engineering" is totally devoid of common law, which is the law of reason in social conduct. This is one purpose of administrative law in a nutshell, to replace the common law. That is why I prefer to term administrative law as phantom law. There is no logical explanation for phantom law's phenomenal growth and expansion in the last eighty odd years. Those that advanced its utilization were lawyers, the elite, and the bureaucratic leadership, then and now.

> *Deceivers do not like the light of truth, and they will fight like the dickens to keep you and anyone else from turning on such a light.*

Phantom law molds a social society that is pliable, manageable, controllable, maneuverable, and yielding, thus docile and passive to the affairs of pseudo government. This goal can only be attained when people stop volunteering into this bizarre administrative law via agencies and regional commissions. This administrative law system has used every scheme and trick in the book to wield its deceptive web of deceit to con the white citizenry into voluntarily trading their birthright in America for some de facto government agency granted and governed privilege.

The only way the courtroom proceedings can be effectively changed is for spectator-clients to open their eyes to the truth of their role in the arena they may find themselves in one day. They must not participate. Learn from the hearing and/or trial of the apostle Paul recorded in Acts 24 through 26 in the New Testament. We must eliminate the deception and replace it with the reality of truth and honesty. Citizens must assert that any accusations be brought against them in a certified court of common law judicial venue and jurisdiction. This type of conduct will have to become an art or science in knowing how *not* to volunteer, but yet assert your organic State citizenship.

To remove darkness from a dark room, you must turn on a light. Deceivers do not like the light of truth, and they will fight like the dickens to keep you and anyone else from turning on such a light. They do not want anyone in their brazen regional system to escape, ever. Remember the zoo in Fort Worth, Texas, and its cage of birds held captive by darkness and deception. This is the very same method employed by the phantom law to keep its subjects/slaves secure.

Why would anyone want to place themselves in the arena of the courtroom scene in the first place? Why would a citizen want to be subject to the administrative law venue and jurisdiction? In today's real world we are often compelled to enter a defensive posture to protect or preserve our position, property, or circumstance. A traffic ticket is possibly the best example. Most folks just go before the judge and pay. Often it's all done through the mail via phone conversations or online. But one must remember that you *voluntarily* went and applied for the license. You pay and everything is fine, you think!

The problem is, how can some entity force or compel performance out of you? How do you fall under the "court's" jurisdiction and in its venue? In simple terms, you granted this illegal system jurisdiction by some voluntary act, such as applying for a license. You can get out the same way. Fraud will not stand the true test of your voluntary act, if in fact such was induced by fraud.

A lot of spectators think or believe that the court always has power over everybody, anywhere. This is not true. This nation was founded on personal freedom, liberty, and justice for all. We, the descendants of the founding fathers, are the sovereigns in this nation of the united States of America. You have to somehow enter the playing field or agree to play the game. You must "invoke" the court's jurisdiction.

To make my point, if you are a spectator at a wrestling match, you do not fall under the same exact rules and regulations that are used to control the wrestlers who are inside the ropes of the small stage in the center of the building. The real arena is inside the perimeter of the ropes. But by placing yourself in the same building of the wrestling match, you implied that you are under the regional administrative law enforced to govern the match. One mistake made in the past has been that we viewed the ring or arena as the only place their law could be enforced. In a larger sense, they have to control all persons in the building where the match takes place or they would have chaos. But the real kicker is that you did not have to attend the match at all—you went voluntarily. You walked into the building to view the match. The same is often true of court.

Until a great awaking surrounding the control and grip that this phantom law has on America is realized, any descendant of the founding fathers who asserts his sovereignty will find himself in a minority and subject to persecution. He must face the fact that most of this nation's people have been duped, deceived, and coddled into a real belief that phantom law, i.e., de facto administrative law, rules most every facet of their individual lives. Their illusive "it's the law" syndrome enslaves most by ignorance, fear, and greed through voluntarism.

In our Constitution for the united States of America (1787) under Article III, there are three jurisdictions that can be invoked in a real court (in court) of justice. In other words, these are the three major playing fields under or onto which you the spectator/citizen can enter or invoke into an active game.

The analogy that best explains these jurisdictions is the contrast of three ball games and their "playing fields" that most everyone is familiar with:

1. Basketball or common law or at law
2. Football or equity law
3. Baseball or admiralty/maritime law

In your minds eye, picture for a minute these three different games and their basic rules and regulations. Remember, they are all ball games—just three different kinds of ball games. They are all played with a different set of rules and regulations.

A full and clear comprehension of how each game is played should result in an understanding as to just how the court's jurisdiction operates with different rules in each jurisdiction (playing field). The rules are different for each. Often the courts attempt to and accomplish a blending of two or more of the systems together. To do such only disrupts and confuses everything and everyone even more. You simply cannot mix the rules for different ball games and continue to play one individual game. The disruption of order only causes the players to become disgusted. Confusion ensues for all concerned.

Think for a minute, how does criminal law affect me if I commit no crimes. The criminal act, which is most often done voluntarily, invokes the aspects of known criminal statutes or common law. In court, the facts of some type of action committed by the person convicts that person for their criminal act. The exposed facts, that you volunteered, brands you as one of their subjects/slaves to be regulated under phantom law.

But "they," the powers that be, came up with an entirely new game. It is termed regional administrative law. Today, this fourth game is in progress. It's an entirely new game. It is the main game and purported to be the only game in town. It now purportedly supersedes all the three above listed games. There is no ball game to pattern this new game after. It combines all rules for all ball games or wrestling matches under an ever changing policy. It is in constant change of its rules. It is tyrannical and abusive in nature. It is the centralization of power in government. The game, i.e., phantom law's goal, is to rule and control society by deceptive tactics, mainly to get everyone who is a free white citizen to simply *volunteer* to be so enslaved. Sound the alarms! It must be stopped! Quite volunteering before the Union known as the American common law Republic, i.e., the united States of America, crumbles into a heap of worthless ash to be trampled under by aliens and/or despots and tyrants.

We need to heed what James Madison penned in 1785: "It is proper to take alarm at the first experiment on our liberties. We hold this prudent jealousy to be the first duty of citizens, and one of the noblest characteristics of the late Revolution. The freeman of America did not wait till usurped power had strengthened itself by exercise, and entangled the question in precedents. They saw all the consequences in the principle, and they avoided the consequences by denying the principle."

It sure seems that today we are beyond the point that Madison so profoundly recollected. Years later another leader issued a warning that needs our undivided attention. Daniel Webster said, "Nothing will ruin the country if the people themselves will undertake its safety; and nothing can save it if they leave that safety in any hand but their own."

In conclusion, I find the words of Chief Justice Story at the end of his book *Commentaries on the Constitution of the United States*, in 1833, the best summation:

> If these Commentaries shall but inspire in the rising generation a more ardent love of their country, an unquenchable thirst for liberty, and a profound reverence for the constitution of the Union, then they will have accomplished all, that their author ought to desire. Let the American youth never forget, that they possess a noble inheritance, bought by the toils, and sufferings, and blood of their ancestors; and capable, if wisely improved, and

faithfully guarded, of transmitting to their latest posterity all the substantial blessings of life, the peaceful enjoyment of liberty, property, religion, and independence. The structure has been erect by architects of consummate skill and fidelity; its foundations are solid; its compartments are beautiful, as well as useful; its arrangements are full of wisdom and order; and its defences are impregnable from without. It has been reared for immortality, if the work of man may justly aspire to such a title. It may, nevertheless, perish in an hour by the folly, or corruption, or negligence of its only keepers, THE PEOPLE. Republics are created by the virtue, public spirit, and intelligence of the citizens. They fall, when the wise are banished from the public councils, because they dare to be honest, and the profligate are rewarded, because they flatter the people, in order to betray them.

"Greater than the tread of mighty armies is an idea whose time has come." ~Victor Hugo, History of a Crime

Epilogue

Just a few days after I finished typing "Phantom Law Rules," I was illegally arrested and unlawfully incarcerated under the guise of a purported administrative law via the forceful arm of martial law. I viewed this as an attempted effort to compel and coerce me into a submission and/or a surrender of my common law status as a free white State citizen and volunteer myself back into phantom law's regional corrupted administrative system.

For twenty days, from December 3, 1991, to December 23, 1991, I was unlawfully deprived of my liberty and freedom in Potter County Correctional Center in Amarillo, Texas, vi et armis. I feel that my research for this book helped prepare me for that unwanted "vacation."

It was through the support of many fine folks and my heavenly Father that I held my ground and would not volunteer. It is my prayer that my experience will help others gain knowledge and understanding on *voluntarism* and how phantom law rule operates.

The government apparently aborted their purported trumped up case number CA 2–91-0059 as the judge signed an "Order Dismissing Summons Enforcement Action Without Prejudice" on February 10, 1992. Praises and thanks to my heavenly Father for this gesture, as the Father has again answered my prayers.

You can read all about this experience in the January 1992 issue of *BEHOLD NEWSLETTER!* in a 50-page article titled "TEXAS CITIZENS K. O. THE I.R.S." with a follow-up article in the February issue. To obtain these issues, you can contact the newsletter by mail or phone:

BEHOLD NEWSLETTER!
Fourth Judicial District
11348 SE 33rd
Milwaukie, Oregon
503–659-6545

Favorite Scriptures

"Many are the afflictions of the righteous: but the Lord delivereth him out of them all" (Ps. 34:19).

"The LORD is my light and my salvation; whom shall I fear? the LORD is the strength of my life; of whom shall I be afraid? When the wicked, even mine enemies and my foes, came upon me to eat up my flesh, they stumbled and fell. Though an host should encamp against me, my heart shall not fear: though war should rise against me, in this will I be confident. One thing have I desired of the LORD, that will I seek after; that I may dwell in the house of the LORD all the days of my life, to behold the beauty of the LORD, and to enquire in his temple. For in the time of trouble he shall hide me in his pavilion: in the secret of his tabernacle shall he hide me; he shall set me up upon a rock" (Ps. 27:1–5).

"He leadeth me in the paths of righteousness for his name's sake" (Ps. 23:3).

"Deliver me from mine enemies, O my God; defend me from them that rise up against me ... for God is my defence" (Ps. 59:1, 9).

"This is the day which the Lord hath made; we will rejoice and be glad in it" (Ps. 118:24).

Additional Materials

The author, Troy D. Barclay, also has other pamphlets available. The titles and topics are as follows:

1. An audio 90-minute recorded lecture titled "Breakers of the Law"
2. A 21-page pamphlet titled "A History of Texas and the Free White Citizen"
3. A 20-page pamphlet titled "Marriage and Divorce and the White Race"

Each of these written documents is an expression for freedom and the restoration of our beloved American Christian common law Republic.

To request these pamphlets, please contact:
Troy D. Barclay
Enthusiasm Plus Ministries
118 South Cedar
Perryton, Ochiltree County, Texas
(Use NO Zip code with the address; it's not a law)

Bibliography

American Dictionary of the English Language. 1828.

American Jurisprudence. San Francisco, CA: Bancroft/Whitney Company; Rochester, NY: The Lawyers Co-operative Publishing, 1936.

American Jurisprudence. 2nd ed. San Francisco, CA: Bancroft/ Whitney Company; Rochester, NY: The Lawyers Co-operative Publishing, 1962.

Behold! Newsletter. Fourth Judicial District, 11348 SE 33rd, Milwaukie, Oregon.

Bevis, Howard, L. *Public Law.* Vol. 3. The National Law Library. New York, NY: P. F. Collier & Son Corporation, 1939.

Black's Law Dictionary. 3rd ed. 1933.

Black's Law Dictionary. 5th ed. 1979.

Bouvier, John. *A Law Dictionary adapted to the Constitution and Laws of the United states of America and of the Several States of the American Union.* Philadelphia, PA:

Childs & Peterson, 1859. The Common Law Course. Universal Life University School of Law. Modesto, CA.

Cox, Mac C. *Fundamentals of Law and Legal Principles.* Minneapolis, MN, and Toronto: Burgess Publishing Company, 1978.

de la Boétie, Étienne. *A Discourse on Voluntary Servitude.* New York, NY: Columbia University Press, 1942.

Edmunds, Sterling E., LL,D. *Struggle for Freedom: The History of Anglo-American Liberty From the Charter of Henry I to the Present Day.* Milwaukee, MN: The Bruce Publishing Company, 1946.

Johnston, Lynn. *Who's Afraid of the IRS?* Fox & Wilkes Books, 1983.

Kowalik, Frank. *IRS Humbug, IRS Weapons of Enslavement.* Oakland Park, FL: Universalistic Publishers, 1991.

Mason, Alpheus Thomas and Donald Grier Stephenson Jr. *American Constitutional Law:*

Introductory Essays and Selected Cases. 9th ed. Englewood Cliffs, NJ: Prentice Hall, 1990.

Story, Joseph, LL.D. *Commentaries on the Constitution of the United States.* Boston, MA: Hilliard, Gray, and Company; Cambridge: Brown, Shattuck, and Co., 1833.

Texas Jurisprudence. 2nd ed. San Francisco, CA: Bancroft/Whitney Company; Rochester, NY: The Lawyers Co-operative Publishing, 1959,

Webster's New Collegiate Dictionary. 1946.

Webster's New Universal Unabridged Dictionary. 2nd ed. 1983.

Appendix A

𝔘nited 𝔖tates 𝔖enate

WASHINGTON, D.C. 20510

December 16, 1981

Mr. Troy Barclay
███████████
Perryton, Texas ███████

Dear Mr. Barclay:

Thank you for contacting my office.

There is no Social Security law requiring that one have a number
but the IRS Tax Code (Section 6109 subsection "a") stipulates that
taxpayers shall utilize their Social Security numbers when filing
tax returns. Therefore, if one pays taxes, one must have a
Social Security number.

If I can be of assistance on another matter, please do not
hesitate to contact my office.

Sincerely,

Lloyd Bentsen

Lloyd Bentsen

Appendix B

SOCIAL SECURITY ADMINISTRATION

BALTIMORE, MARYLAND 21235

RECEIVED

2·28·81

REFER TO: SPP—A1

■■■■■

Mr. Troy Duwayne Barclay

■■■■■

Perryton, Texas ■■■■■

Dear Mr. Barclay:

We are returning your request for full payment from your social security record.

There is no provision in the Social Security Act which would permit a person to receive cash settlements from his or her social security contributions. The social security program is not a plan that guarantees the return of the person's social security contributions. It is a system of social insurance under which employees, their employers, and self-employed people who are engaged in work covered by the program pay social security contributions to provide insurance protection for individuals and their families. This insures against the risk of loss of income from work because of retirement, disability, or death, and against hospital care costs for people 65 and older and some people under 65 who are disabled. Contributions paid on a person's earnings are not allocated specifically to his or her social security record. Instead, they are pooled in special funds from which benefit payments are made to those persons (and their families) who have worked long enough to be insured and who have incurred the risk against which the program provides insurance.

If you wish further information, you should get in touch with your Internal Revenue Service office.

Sincerely yours,

Barbara P. Smith

Social Insurance Claims Examiner
Office of Central Records Operations

Enclosure

108

Appendix C

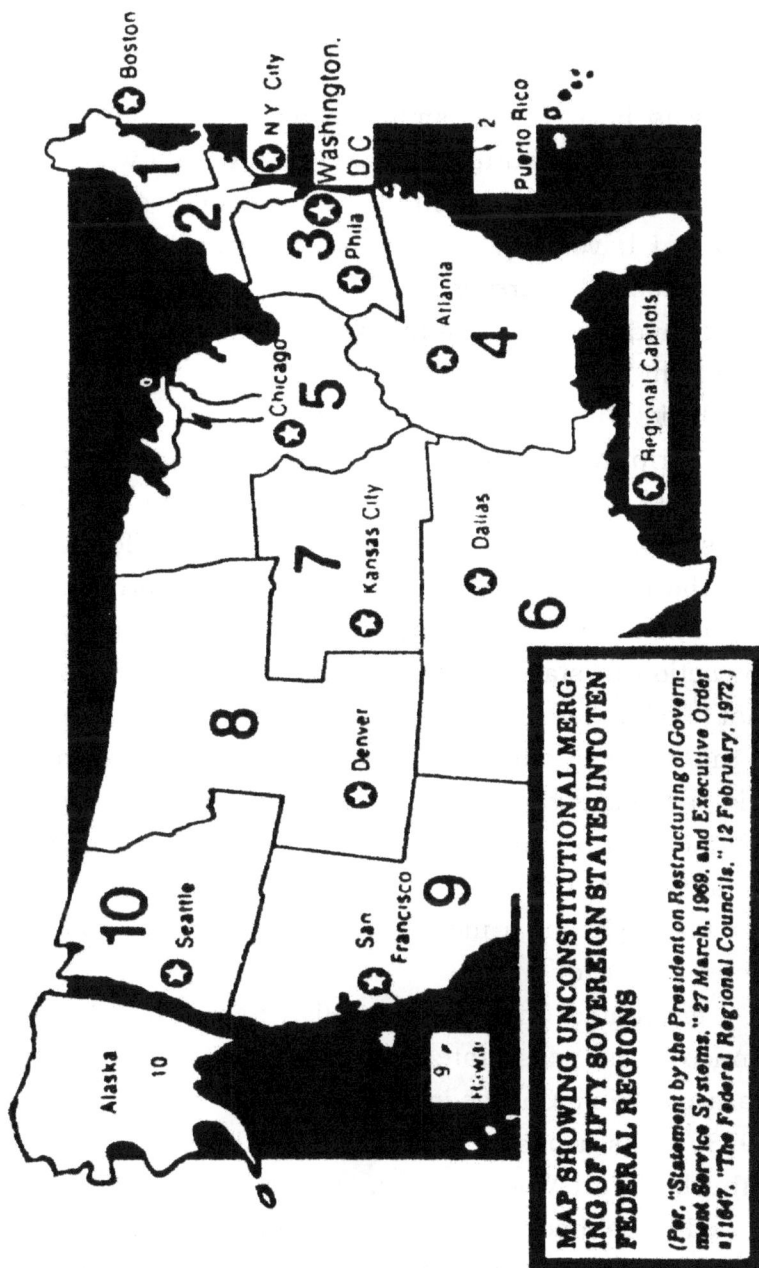

MAP SHOWING UNCONSTITUTIONAL MERGING OF FIFTY SOVEREIGN STATES INTO TEN FEDERAL REGIONS

(Per, "Statement by the President on Restructuring of Government Service Systems," 27 March, 1969, and Executive Order #11647, "The Federal Regional Councils," 12 February, 1972.)

Regional Capitols

Boston — 1
NY City — 2
Washington, D.C.
Phila — 3
Atlanta — 4
Chicago — 5
Dallas — 6
Kansas City — 7
Denver — 8
San Francisco — 9
Seattle — 10
Alaska — 10
Hawaii — 9
Puerto Rico — 2

About the Author

I was born in the small Texas panhandle town of Perryton in the County of Ochiltree in 1943. I was raised in that small rural community and encouraged to be self-reliant. I have been married to my wife, LaDonna, for more than 48 years. We have four children and eleven grandchildren. I have supported my family without any help from "Big Brother."

I believe in the morals and principles set forth in the Holy Scriptures of the God of Israel. I have attempted to be honest, fair, and just in all my dealings in life. Jesus Christ is my Savior and Guide. I believe in life, liberty, and the pursuit of happiness. I cannot compromise my convictions, nor do I want too. I am compelled by this conviction to stand for the freedom, liberty, and justice that I believe was bequeathed to this land by the founders of this nation. I will never give up my fight to restore the original and organic Constitutional American Christian common law Republic and all law not repugnant thereto. We are being tricked, on every front, to voluntarily trade our birthright for a mere government granted and protected privilege.

I graduated from Perryton High School in 1962, attended West Texas State University, and graduated from Nazarene Bible College in Colorado Springs, Colorado, in 1973. I was a pastor in the city of White Settlement, a suburb of Fort Worth, Texas, from 1973 to 1975. I then moved to Lubbock, Texas, in 1975 and was self-supporting in a garage venture until the death of my dad in 1979.

I then moved the garage venture back to Perryton. I was elected constable of Justice Precinct One in 1984 and served for four years in that position. Ochiltree County had not had an active constable in some forty years.

I then went on to receive a doctor of common law degree from the Universal Life University School of Common Law correspondence program in Modesto, California, in 1984. I am involved in numerous court battles to restore this land to organic law under the Republic. I love to share and lecture.

We invite you to view the complete
selection of titles we publish at:

www.AspectBooks.com

Scan with your mobile
device to go directly
to our website.

Please write or email us your praises, reactions, or
thoughts about this or any other book we publish at:

AB ASPECT Books
www.ASPECTBooks.com

P.O. Box 954
Ringgold, GA 30736

info@AspectBooks.com

Aspect Books titles may be purchased in bulk for
educational, business, fund-raising, or sales promotional use.
For information, please e-mail:

BulkSales@AspectBooks.com

Finally, if you are interested in seeing
your own book in print, please contact us at:

publishing@AspectBooks.com

We would be happy to review your manuscript for free.

www.ingramcontent.com/pod-product-compliance
Lightning Source LLC
Chambersburg PA
CBHW071453200326
41519CB00019B/5722